Len,

Your commitment to your customers and understanding the concepts in this is core to the concepts in this is core to the

Keep on focusing on your customers!

CUSTOMER-CENTRIC PRODUCT DEFINITION

The Key to Great Product Development

Sheila Mello

AMACOM
American Management Association
New York · Atlanta · Brussels · Buenos Aires · Chicago · London · Mexico City · San Francisco
Shanghai · Tokyo · Toronto · Washington, DC

This publication is designed to provide accurate and authoritative information
in regard to the subject matter covered. It is sold with the understanding that
the publisher is not engaged in rendering legal, accounting, or other
professional service. If legal advice or other expert assistance is required, the
services of a competent professional person should be sought.

Library of Congress-Cataloging-in-Publication Data

Mello, Sheila, 1943–
    Customer-centric product definition : the key to great product development / Sheila Mello.
        p. cm.
    Includes index.
    ISBN 0-8144-0668-8
    1. New products—Planning.   2. Customer relations.   I. Title

TS171.4 .M45 2001
658.5'75—dc21   2001041378

Printing number

10   9   8   7   6   5   4   3   2   1

I dedicate this book to the past, current, and future clients and colleagues of Product Development Consulting, Inc.,

and to my husband and partner, Larry Smetana.

Contents

Appendix 189

References 213

Index 219

Preface

My passion for understanding customer requirements started very early in my career. In 1967 I was a project leader assigned to develop an order entry, sales analysis, and invoicing system for Cool Ray Sun Glasses, a division of American Optical. I didn't know anything about the optical business, and in fact I had never taken an accounting course! So, instead of relying on my own training or expertise, I went out and talked to the customer staff in each department affected. I asked questions, probed, got examples, and took copious notes. After distilling all the information, I designed the system, then held several review sessions with the customers. At the customer acceptance meeting, my client, the vice president of operations for American Optical, said, "Sheila, you are clairvoyant—this meets our needs perfectly, even some we hadn't known we had."

Without realizing it, I had discovered the essence of a process to create a successful product. After many years of fine-tuning the approach, I was introduced to Concept Engineering at the Center for Quality Management. As I discovered what Gary Burchill had developed in Concept Engineering, I found that the process I had been evolving all these years took a similar form. A couple of years later, I joined John Carter at Product Development Consulting, Inc. (PDC), and started a practice area focused on helping companies define their customer requirements and create product strategies and products to speed time to profit. The Market-Driven Product Definition (MDPD®) process evolved as my partners and I implemented MDPD with dozens of companies.

The answers these companies seek are to be found with their customers. I look forward to future work that further refines our understanding of how to help deliver products, services, and solutions that surprise and delight even the most demanding consumers. I challenge you to become a more demanding consumer—and a more sensitive producer—as a result of reading this book.

WHO SHOULD READ THIS BOOK?

For companies that want to increase their market share by offering winning products and services, this book is designed to help individuals in any functional area understand their company's customers and potential customers. Executives will benefit from reading this book by developing a thorough understanding of the product definition process. The book will help guide their decisions before, during, and after they implement a development project or program; they will see how their decisions affect their company's product development activities. Individuals and teams who are directly involved in the product development process will benefit from the road map for creating a robust and thorough product definition process that the book provides. This book is also must reading for anyone involved in marketing or sales functions. The tremendous marketing power generated from truly understanding customer requirements is a company differentiator in itself and can be a significant competitive advantage. Finally, professors should include this book as required reading for students in engineering and business curricula.

Acknowledgments

This book was in no small measure due to the dedication of our customers, who helped us explore the ins and outs of the process and allowed us to learn from their experiences.

We would like to thank all of the companies we have worked with to implement Market-Driven Product Definition over the past decade, either for specific projects or for divisionwide or companywide standard practices. We would especially like to thank those individuals we interviewed and those who informally contributed their and their company's experiences with the MDPD process. Their quotes may or may not have made it into the final version; however, their input shaped every aspect of the book. Our special thanks goes to the following individuals: Roy Armstrong, Dade Behring, Inc.; Steve Binder, Bio-Rad Laboratories, Inc.; Chris Bohrson, Teradyne, Inc.; Jim Cournoyer, Honeywell, Inc.; Robert Crecsenzi, formerly with Compaq Computer Corporation; Tim Erickson, Honeywell, Inc.; Denise Flinn, Teradyne, Inc.; Michael L. Grant, The Chinet Company; Glenn House, formerly with Mentor Graphics Corporation; Carole Katz, Avaya, Inc.; David LaDuke, formerly with Linuxcare, Inc.; Derek Lehane, formerly with Dade Behring, Inc.; Mary McDaniels, Kimberly-Clark Corporation; William Naccarato, Dade Behring, Inc.; Carmen Najork, Becton Dickinson and Company; Dev Nanda, Reynolds & Reynolds Company; Cheryl Perkins, Kimberly-Clark Corporation; Dawn Piacentino, Educational Testing Service; George Powell, Educational Testing Service; Ken Reindel, formerly with Keithley Instruments, Inc.; Buzz Sztukowski, bioMerieux; Len Swanson, Educational Testing Service; Robert Thomson, formerly with Compaq Computer Corporation; Tag Van Winkle, Abbott Laboratories; Barbara Vilkomerson, Educational Testing Service; and Betsy Westlake, Kimberly-Clark Corporation.

Special thanks also go to the following companies, whose enthusiasm has helped us evolve the process as we helped them implement it: Abbott Laboratories; Agilent Technologies; Avaya, Inc.; Becton Dickinson and Company; bioMerieux, Inc.; Bio-Rad, Inc.; C.R. Bard, Inc.; Cisco Systems; Compaq Computer Corporation; Dade Behring, Inc.; Eastman Kodak Company; Educational Testing Service; Honeywell, Inc.; Intermec Corporation; IPC Information Systems; JLG Industries, Inc.; Keithley Instruments, Inc.; LDM Technologies; Linuxcare, Inc.; Lucent Technologies; Medtronic, Inc.; Mentor Graphics Corporation; New Pig; Reynolds & Reynolds, Inc.; Teradyne Corporation; Tektronix, Inc.; The Chinet Company; The Nasdaq Stock Market, Inc.; Stanley Works Corporation; and Western Digital Corporation.

When we decided that an appendix containing a full example of the process would be valuable to the reader, we called on our golfing family and friends to provide customer input. Many thanks to Gerry DiBiassi, Lyse Fontaine, Bruce Greenberg, Barry Liner, Bob Neumeyer, Dick Peppin, and Paul Smetana for investing their time to help us.

Creating a process such as MDPD is an iterative journey that evolved from collaborative sessions among people with whom I have been fortunate to work during my tenure at PDC. David Boger, John Carter, Scott Elliott, Lyse Fontaine, Alan Graham, Warren Harkness, Ron Lasser, and Wayne Mackey all contributed their unique skills and knowledge to the growth of the process.

The book would not have happened without Audrey Kalman's countless hours of editing, rewriting, and encouragement.

On a more personal note, I would like to thank my devoted husband, Larry Smetana, for all the insight and patience he has had in the preparation of this book. His marketing expertise and business experience lent insights from a discipline that complemented my background. We worked as a team, and from the very start, the book would not have been possible without his support. I owe much of the material to his interest, and I look forward to many more evenings spent discussing the benefits of customer-centric thinking and acting.

INTRODUCTION: MARKET-DRIVEN PRODUCT DEFINITION

The Key to Defuzzing the Fuzzy Front End

IF YOU DON'T KNOW WHERE YOU'RE GOING, YOU'LL NEVER GET THERE

In June of 1998, Circuit City Stores introduced Divx (Digital Video Express), a pay-per-view variant of DVD (digital versatile disk), in limited release in San Francisco, California, and in Virginia. A Divx disk would work only in a Divx recorder connected to the telephone. Buyers of these special recorders and disks could register to play a disk for forty-eight hours. However, after forty-eight hours, the disk became unplayable. The customer would then either throw away the disk or register with Circuit City for an additional viewing through the modem in the recorder, with the $3.25 fee charged to a credit card. This eliminated the nuisance of returning the disk (but also contributed to landfill).

In June of 1999, Circuit City pulled the plug on Divx and wrote it off as a $114 million loss. Had Circuit City ever known where it was going?

1

IF YOU DON'T ASK THE CUSTOMER, YOU'LL PROBABLY GO TO THE WRONG PLACE

Divx was not dreamed up by an engineer disconnected from reality; the concept was developed by a Hollywood entertainment-law firm. What went wrong?

Circuit City and its partners developed the special video hardware and software and waited for customers to embrace their clever idea. The benefits of Divx for investors, promoters, and distributors were clearly perceived, but *the benefits for the potential customer were not*. The disk couldn't be used in a friend's conventional DVD player. Nor could you pop it into a laptop computer during a long flight instead of watching an exciting in-flight movie. The value to the customer could not have been the primary criterion for the development of the Divx system. It was not apparent how the needs of potential customers would be addressed before, during, and after the purchase of the Divx system. As Jim Porter of industry newsletter *DiskTrend* commented, "Everyone remembers Beta vs. VHS . . . [Circuit City did not consider the] point of view of the suffering customers."[1] Like many so-called push technologies and ill-conceived product development programs, the Divx venture was dead on arrival.

The Value of a Customer-Centric Focus

Before William F. Peare founded Trendwest Resorts, Inc., in 1989, he spent nine months interviewing potential customers to try to determine exactly what they were looking for in a vacation. What his research revealed was that people were not taking as many once-a-year–vacations; instead they were opting for more frequent, shorter retreats several times a year. His in-depth research led to the development of a strategy centered on locating resorts within a two- to five-hour drive from major metropolitan areas and selling vacation credits rather than vacation weeks. Instead of locking owners into one week at the same resort in the same unit (typical with time sharing), Trendwest set up a system of vacation credits that could be applied toward vacations at resorts in six western areas, including Hawaii, British Columbia, and Mexico. This would allow a family to take shorter, more frequent vacations within an easy drive of home.

In October of 1989, Trendwest's resorts consisted of two condominium developments in the Pacific Northwest. A decade later, the resort network includes thirty-one locations with 1,635 luxury condominiums. Revenues and earnings have kept pace. Revenues increased to a record $338 million and earnings rose to a record $2.53 per share in 2000.

Trendwest is focused on the customer to such an extent that computer screens at the operation's reservation center display the message "Never say no." The message is intended to remind reservation operators never to deny a customer request if it is at all reasonable. Providing superior customer satisfaction through the combination of quality accommodations, maintenance, and customer service also separates Trendwest from the rest of the resort industry. Giving customers what they want is nothing new, but Peare's research proved the value of understanding what customers want before they know it themselves.[2]

PUTTING FIRST THINGS FIRST: STARTING WITH THE PRODUCT DEFINITION PROCESS TO CLOSE THE CUSTOMER-CENTRICITY GAP

The key to product success is paradoxically simple: Delight the customer by creating a product that fills a specific need in the marketplace better than competing solutions. The simplicity of this idea belies the complexity of actually carrying it out.

The problems that lead to product failures like Divx are not new. For years, companies have sought to improve profitability by adopting the business management strategies and philosophies *du jour*. But most of these strategies and philosophies place the company and its prod-ucts—not the customers' requirements—at the epicenter.

Contemporary authors, consultants, and top management spout phrases such as *customer orientation, customer-driven, listening to the voice of the customer, becoming more customer-centric, customer awareness,* and *customer retention* to emphasize that the customer and the market drive the business. In reality, however, there is a yawning gap between how well senior managers *think* they address customer concerns and how well they actually do so, creating what could be called a customer-centricity gap.[3] With these inaccurate perceptions of their companies' commitment to customers, senior management can hardly be expected to support additional efforts to systematically identify customer needs. Further-more, the variables related to customer-centricity are somewhat amor-phous and difficult, if not impossible, to measure, whereas quality can be quantified and easily measured through defects, yield, warranty repairs, returns, and customer complaints. This helps explain why companies have not put forth the same herculean effort to address the customer-centricity gap that they expend to conquer quality problems.

Closing the customer-centricity gap must start with the adoption of a customer-centric product definition process. Unfortunately, current literature offers little guidance as to how to identify and capture cus-tomer requirements and translate those requirements into successful products—in other words, how to define the product. Most existing books discuss the phases of the product development process (prototyp-ing, manufacturing, testing) that follow product definition. But the prob-lem begins much earlier, at the front end of the product development process—the period during which companies conceptualize and plan the product. Even books that address market definition and market research fail to bridge the gap, in a practical way, between research about what customers want and defining a product that provides this.

Clearly, a product development methodology that hopes to address this thorny problem *must* put first things first and clarify the earliest stages of the product development process, during which the company decides what product it will create and for whom, and what features will entice customers to buy the product.

Product Development Consulting, Inc. (PDC), a firm devoted to helping companies optimize processes throughout the product life cycle, from strategy to product retirement, has worked with companies in a wide range of industries since 1990. Its consultants have seen the inside of the product development process at hundreds of companies. Based on this experience, PDC has developed an approach that not only bridges the enormous gap between theory and practice, but also begins where the process must: at the very beginning.

WHAT MAKES MDPD DIFFERENT?

Unlike other methodologies, PDC's Market-Driven Product Definition (MDPD®) process is customer-centric. It begins *before* the development process gets underway, at the logical starting point: the customer. It addresses the customer's requirements in a systematic, analytical, and repeatable way to generate a product definition that will lead to innovative product solutions, with attendant measurable results for companies.

The MDPD process provides concrete data to help companies allocate their resources in a way that maximizes returns. It uses a fact-based methodology to demystify and define what is often referred to as the fuzzy front end of product development. The MDPD approach is particularly relevant when one considers the all-too-common gap between engineering and marketing in determining product requirements. MDPD helps companies avoid unnecessarily changing product requirements, so-called creeping elegance or feature creep. The methodology places the data collection, processing, and analysis work in the hands of a cross-functional team of product developers to improve the clarity of requirements and enhance the credibility of the solutions created to meet those requirements.

Studies confirm that PDC clients using the MDPD techniques exhibit significantly lower levels of misdirected effort, fewer product specification changes, and higher degrees of design problem resolution. The results have been to decrease time to market (in some cases up to 40 percent compared to those programs not employing this customer-centric approach), thereby saving companies money and often accounting for the difference between being a market leader and being a laggard.

PDC client companies also report a marked improvement in market acceptance of new products defined with the MDPD process. Recently, a well-known U.S. consumer electronics manufacturer, using the processes and tools embodied in MDPD, introduced the most successful product, as measured by dollar sales volume, unit volume, and profit contribution, in its thirty-two-year history. PDC clients report improvements in their research and development (R&D) effectiveness as measured by sales growth attributable to products introduced within the past two years, coincident with the regular use of the MDPD method.

A robust and well-executed customer-centric product definition process not only identifies the obvious voice of the customer, but also, more importantly, helps to identify the customer's *unstated* or latent needs. PDC's MDPD process uses in-context market research and customer visits to help clarify the customer's definition of value. The methodology draws on well-established principles in concept engineering[4] and customer visits,[5] which were developed and refined both by PDC and by respected product development consultants and academics from the Massachusetts Institute of Technology, the University of Chicago, and the Center for the Management of Quality. The inch-wide, mile-deep structure of the methodology, which deeply and exhaustively probes customers, helps answer the trickiest product development questions:

- What are the meaningful customer/market requirements for a new or enhanced product?
- Which customer-value-based requirements should the product development effort target in order to create competitive differentiation in the market?
- What trade-offs can be made in the product development process, and how will these affect the product?
- What product features represent value for customers and which will exceed customer expectations, resulting in delighted customers?
- How should a company invest its resources in developing particular product features to satisfy customer-value-based needs?
- Exactly what product features or attributes should the solution set include?

- Which customer requirements need only be equivalent to competitive offerings in the market to avoid adversely affecting projected market capture?

WHAT'S IN THE REST OF THE BOOK?

This book describes how MDPD, as a customer-centric product definition process, helps companies develop successful products. Drawing upon thousands of hours of direct experience with PDC's clients and hundreds of hours of follow-up interviews, the book helps people involved in their companies' product development processes, from senior strategists to marketing managers, understand what it takes to develop successful products. The book is *not* intended to be a how-to manual for executing the MDPD process. You will come away with an understanding of the process, what is required to implement it, and whether it will potentially benefit your company.

Chapter 1 presents the case for using a customer-centric product definition. Insights from historical examples of product successes and failures expose the crying need for an analytical process at the fuzzy front end of the product development process. Most companies do not give appropriate attention to this phase of the process, as confirmed by a PDC study.

Chapter 2 discusses the factors that are essential for successful implementation of the MDPD process. Most companies today use some form of customer input as part of the development process. The key factor determining whether product development efforts succeed or fail is the process used to determine customer requirements. The inside-out product orientation that is prevalent in many companies can doom the product development effort before it even begins. MDPD, of which an overview is given in this chapter, is a sixteen-step process that delivers tangible results, documented by actual case histories in various industries.

Chapter 3 outlines the development of a visit matrix and the factors that go into deciding which customers to interview as part of the process. The development of the visit matrix is a central step in the product definition process. It defines the market segment(s) targeted for the development effort and drives the scope, time required, and expense of the product definition effort by identifying which customers are included in customer visits.

Chapter 4 presents the tangible value, supported by case studies, of interviewing customers in their work environments. It also introduces the concept of the customer image as a valuable means of understanding the true voice of the customer. It presents interview guidelines and principles, and the necessity of role playing for the interview process.

Chapter 5 builds on the idea of the customer image as a tool for creating a customer-centric product definition. Successfully identifying the image of the customer in the customer's environment allows the development team to conceive of products from the customer's perspective.

Chapter 6 is structured around the theme of identifying customer requirements. Translating customers' multivalued language into tangible requirements is not a simple, straightforward process. The chapter describes the process of separating the must-have from the me-too features and defining the elements that will delight customers.

Chapter 7 establishes the criticality of developing metrics to ensure that customer requirements have been identified and are being properly evaluated. It provides the insight for identifying which customer requirements the product development effort will address. It provides objective criteria to measure product development concepts and trade-offs. Developing a requirement/metric matrix allows the team to select the requirements to address and provides a customer-centric basis on which to differentiate the planned product or service.

Chapter 8 discusses the difficult task of validating and prioritizing customer requirements and selecting which of these requirements to address. The concepts presented in this chapter allow a company to evaluate customer requirements objectively.

Chapter 9 presents the approaches necessary to thoroughly evaluate competitive offerings in the market, using a weighted concept selection matrix for product positioning. The chapter presents technology and price/performance mapping and discusses the identification of technological drivers to measure against customer requirements and competitive offerings.

Chapter 10 explores methodologies for generating, screening, and selecting product concepts and presents several techniques that can help the reader develop product specifications.

Chapter 11 looks at methods for evaluating the product concepts generated in Chapter 10, with an eye toward choosing those that provide the most value to customers and a tolerable level of risk to the company.

Chapter 12 looks to the future and the impact of the Internet on product definition. It examines how companies can let their customers lead the way to optimizing the product definition using the Web.

The appendix shows the flow of the MDPD process from beginning to end, using a fictional case study involving a company that produces golf bags.

I

THE CASE FOR MARKET-DRIVEN PRODUCT DEFINITION

The Universal Problem

> Midway through her adventures in Wonderland, Alice asked the Cheshire Cat which way she ought to go.
> "That depends a good deal on where you want to get to," said the Cat.
> "I don't much care where—" said Alice.
> "Then it doesn't matter which way you go," said the Cat.
> "—so long as I get SOMEWHERE," Alice added as an explanation.
> "Oh, you're sure to do that," said the Cat, "if you only walk long enough."
>
> —From Alice's Adventures in Wonderland,
> by Lewis Carroll

The landscape of unsuccessful product developments is littered with the remains of seemingly clever ideas that never quite made it. This certainly is not a new phenomenon, and it has been a dominant concern of business executives for decades. We can learn a lot from history, but unfortunately many companies have not taken those lessons to heart, or don't have the tools at hand to do so. The failure of Ford Motor Company's

Edsel, for example, has become a part of business and cultural lore. Looking deeper into the reasons behind that failure offers valuable lessons for students of a customer-centric product definition process.

THE EDSEL VS. THE MUSTANG

Since the development and introduction of the Edsel on September 4, 1957, the word *Edsel* has become synonymous with failure. The sales goal for model year 1958 was set at 200,000 cars. In July of 1957, full-scale production of the Edsel began. On November 30, 1957, Henry Ford II told Edsel dealers, "Gentlemen, the Edsel is here to stay." In January of 1958, Ford formed the Mercury-Edsel-Lincoln Division. That year, the company delivered 63,110 Edsels, falling short of its sales goal by more than 68 percent.

The Edsel had many features that were innovative for the time and that have since become standard, such as self-adjusting brakes, an electronic hood release, and the ability to lock the transmission in park until the ignition is engaged. However, these features did not add up to a car that buyers wanted. The Edsel's styling, while unique, failed to appeal to a substantial number of potential buyers.

Ford's decision to highlight the Edsel's powerful engine during a period when the buying public was gravitating toward smaller, more fuel-efficient cars alienated potential customers. The first models in the showroom were the most expensive, top-of-the-line models, resulting in what we refer to today as sticker shock. Unfortunately, too, while some Edsel models were more expensive than comparable cars, they had an equivalent or greater number of quality problems. Often parts did not fit properly or were simply missing, since Ford frequently built Edsels between Fords and Mercurys on the same assembly line. Many dealers were ill equipped to replace these parts or add accessories.

Ford introduced 1959 and 1960 model Edsels, but sales plummeted to 44,891 and 2,846 cars, respectively. The November 21, 1959, edition of the *Saturday Evening Post* magazine ran the last ad for the Edsel, and Ford mercifully discontinued the Edsel that same month.

A very different scenario played out only a few years later, when Lee Iacocca, then with Ford, recognized a large and growing market segment of car buyers: affluent families shopping for a second car. Rather than simply creating a car, Ford wanted to understand customer desires and the value of the proposed car to the potential customer. That way, the company could develop a product that would tap the sweet spot in this market.

Ford turned to its market researchers, and the market researchers went to the customers. The market researchers identified growth in the number of families owning two cars, with the second car smaller and sportier than the family car. They also discovered that more women and single people were buying new cars. They then defined the necessary or must-have requirements for this new product. The new car must have strong performance, the capacity to handle four passengers, fuel economy, and a low price. Based on this research, Ford introduced the Falcon, which had many of these features.

But something was missing. The Ford market researchers went back and analyzed the buying patterns of Falcon customers. Many of the customers were ordering sportier options, such as automatic transmissions, whitewall tires, and more powerful engines. Ford used this extensive customer research, combined with customer visits, to develop a set of features that would *delight* the customer, not just meet basic expectations. The result was the Ford Mustang, whose final styling featured a long hood and short rear deck with Ferrari flair, giving the appearance of stealth performance—even just sitting in the driveway.

Fifty-two couples with average incomes who already owned a standard-size car were invited to the Ford styling room for a focus group test. Both white-collar and blue-collar couples were impressed with the styling of the Mustang prototype. However, when asked directly whether they would buy a Mustang, most said that they would not—until they learned the proposed price. At a base price of less than $2,500, any potential objections vanished.

WHAT FORD LEARNED FROM THE EDSEL EXPERIENCE

The Mustang was a huge hit. Following on the heels of the extremely successful Falcon, the Mustang was introduced in April of 1964 and sold a record 418,812 vehicles its first year in production, surpassing the Falcon's 417,714-vehicle record. The J. Walter Thompson advertising agency heavily promoted the Mustang. Walter Murphy, of Ford's public relations organization, supported it with press releases, print and media advertising, direct mail, displays, and a plethora of news coverage, including simultaneous appearances on the covers of *Time* and *Newsweek*. During its first two years in production, the Mustang product line generated net profits of $1.1 billion in 1965 dollars. Today, the Mustang appears to be still galloping along and is celebrating its thirty-fifth anniversary in production.

The success of the Mustang demonstrates that Ford Motor Company did learn from the Edsel experience. The key difference between the ill-fated development of the Edsel and the roaring success of the Mustang was the shift from a product-centric focus to a customer-centric one. In his autobiography, Lee Iacocca summed up the differences between Ford's two new car introductions, which came fewer than ten years apart and provided a study in contrasts: "Whereas the Edsel had been a car in search of a market it never found, here was a market in search of a car. The normal procedure in Detroit was to build a car and then try to identify its buyers. But we were in a position to move in the opposite direction—and tailor a new product for a hungry new market."[1]

The success of the Mustang is legendary. Of course, it did benefit from favorable economic conditions, rising disposable income, a soon-to-be-enacted congressional income tax cut, and a burgeoning shift in population created by the baby-boom generation. However, similar conditions exist today, and Circuit City nonetheless experienced a financial disaster as a result of the Divx fiasco. (Recall that Divx, a pay-per-view variant of DVD, was taken off the market by Circuit City less than a year after its introduction, with losses tallying approximately $114 million.) The fundamental difference between the two developments was the process used to define the product. For Divx, the focus was *product-centric* and concentrated only on the financial rewards that would accrue from successful acceptance of the Divx format by the consumer. For the Mustang, the focus was the customer. Thoroughly understanding the customer's stated and unstated values allowed Ford to develop the product to meet those needs and assure its success before introducing it to the customer.

The payoff of the customer-focused approach is unarguable. At the time of the Mustang's introduction, development of an all-new car cost between $300 and $400 million. Ford's cost to develop the Mustang, however, was only $75 million, since many components were the same as those for the Falcon. Ford made $1.1 billion in net profit on its investment in the first two years, while Circuit City lost $114 million.

THE CUSTOMER DRIVES THE DEFINITION OF THE PRODUCT

More than three decades have passed since the introduction of the Mustang. While Ford Motor Company built a number of unspectacular automobiles in the 1970s, it launched the record-breaking Taurus in 1986 and the successful Explorer a few years later. Business paradigms during this period have changed, but the fundamental truth remains: *The customer drives the definition of the product. The organization must adapt its structures, roles, and internal activities to the dynamic requirements of the customer.*

It seems obvious that replicating Mustang product development experiences and avoiding Edsel or Divx experiences ought to be one of a company's primary goals. Why, then, has management theory from the post-World War II era to the present focused not on the customer, but on internal operational efficiency and product-centric issues?

In the years immediately following World War II, there was a tremendous pent-up demand for homes, consumer durable and nondurable goods, services, and virtually anything else that industry was capable of producing. Faced with unprecedented demand, the goal of business was production. The United States was preeminent, and U.S. industry held a monopolistic advantage over the decimated economies of Europe and Japan. The only customer consideration was that customers keep doing what they should do—consume.

The subsequent reindustrialization of Europe and Japan and the competitive threats represented by these economies shifted the focus of U.S. businesses to strategic planning.

It's useful to examine the evolution of market-driven strategy throughout this period to the present. The strategic planning period covered the late 1960s and the decade of the 1970s. During this period, companies focused on improving their financial performance through optimal resource allocation to respond to the growing competitive threat. Each business was evaluated in the context of the corporate strategic plan. However, the limitations of the strategic planning process disappointed many managers. Corporations like General Electric abandoned the strategic planning model and eliminated strategic planning departments in their organizations.[2] In hindsight, it appears that many U.S. businesses were looking through the wrong end of the telescope, focusing on their own products and internal operations.

During the late 1970s and throughout the 1980s, pressures from Japanese industries, which were emerging as world-class competitors, increased. The shift from focusing on strategic planning to maximizing operational efficiency began with—and was led by—the management philosophy emanating from industry practices in Japan. Japanese management theory and practice focused on total quality, just-in-time manufacturing, automation, lights-out manufacturing, and operational efficiency throughout the organization. The emergence of "Japan, Inc." and the new Japanese mantra hit U.S. businesses like Pearl Harbor revisited. This wake-up call resulted in U.S. businesses' wholesale adoption of the total quality management (TQM) philosophy, Deming Quality Awards, organizational restructuring, quality circles, corporate downsizing, rightsizing, and lean and flat management structures. These measures did reduce costs and improve operational effectiveness, but they did not generate growth.

Early in the 1990s, many U.S. businesses, having successfully survived the Japanese threat of the 1980s, began shifting the fundamental premise of their management strategies to a market-driven focus. However, although today most companies consider themselves to be market-driven, many still are not. The problem may be endemic to success itself. During start-up, a company pays close attention to its customers. The very survival of the organization requires intimate knowledge of customer needs and trends. However, as the organization and its customer base expand, the organizational focus tends to shift from customers and their requirements to the company's internal operation. Budgets, core competencies, operational efficiency, and resource allocation become management's chief concerns. Total quality management, reengineering, and quality function deployment may show companies how to operate more cost-effectively, efficiently, and successfully, but the company's very success leads to the integration of these processes and procedures. The result: Companies often develop unwanted, unsuccessful, competitively inferior, or me-too products. This applies equally to the large *Fortune* 500 companies and to mature smaller organizations.

THE PRODUCT DEVELOPMENT PROCESS HOLDS THE KEY

Regardless of the size of your organization, the industry in which you participate, your market share, your growth rate, your profitability, your shareholder value, your growth in market cap, or any other measurement of business success, you face competition (that is, unless you occupy a monopoly position and your customers have no choice but to consume your products or services now and forever). Even companies like Microsoft, the 800-pound gorilla of its market, face competitive threats. Microsoft must stay in front of the competitive technological curve, the Internet, and ward off the U.S. Department of Justice to maintain dominance.

Given the reality of continuous competitive threats, a company's principal business functions, espoused by Peter F. Drucker, are to *innovate* and to *market*. The ability to grow sales, stay ahead of the competition, increase market share, increase profitability, enhance ROI, grow shareholder value, and pursue many other worthwhile business goals begins with innovation through successful product development. Product development is the common element across all companies.

PRODUCT DECISIONS MUST COME BEFORE DEVELOPMENT

It is therefore imperative that an organization make the right product decisions before launching into full-scale product development. Yet many products fail to satisfy their intended customers. Why? Because companies fail to build into the product development process the necessary steps that will ensure the full consideration of customer requirements, both stated and unstated, *before* product development begins.

A study on the factors influencing effective product development conducted by Product Developing Consulting, Inc., and the Management Roundtable reveals the haphazard way in which many companies approach gathering and quantifying customer input. The survey polled 4,000 companies representing a wide cross section of industries[3] selling products that ranged in price from less than $100 to more than $2 million. Products from approximately half of the 335 responding companies sold for less than $1,500.

Only 25 percent of the responding companies fell into the best-in-class group based on the following criteria:

- Their new products met or exceeded sales objectives and financial criteria.

- They had self-reported medium and rising market share, high market share that remained constant, or high and rising market share.

- They felt that their product development process was successful.

- They indicated that products brought new ideas to the market with a shorter cycle time than their competitors.

The remaining companies (close to 250 of them) did not meet these criteria. The results of the survey indicate that both the average and best performers have ample room for improvement in product development.

Although a thorough understanding of customers' needs is an obvious condition for sound product development, fewer than half of all respondents reported that the development team thoroughly understood users' needs at the start of full-scale development.

Digging deeper into the survey results reveals more about the tremendous impact that the appropriate discovery of customer requirements can have on product success. For example, the companies that participated in the PDC study reported that average cycle time for product development in their industries ranged from fifteen to thirty-four months, representing a significant investment in time and cost. Yet the primary cause of major feature changes for all companies, both best and worst in class, was reported to be the *late discovery of customer requirements*. The second highest cause was reported to be unanticipated technical difficulties. While the latter may not be predictable at the start of a project, discovering customer requirements *after* the start of product development is certainly preventable. Unfortunately, the study could not identify how many technical difficulties arose as a result of late discovery of customer requirements.

The same two factors, late discovery of customer requirements and technical difficulties, were cited as causes of schedule slips, which can have a devastating effect on time to market. Not surprisingly, the best companies had lower slip rates in their planned product development than the rest. About 35 percent of the companies in the remaining group reported experiencing slippage in their product development schedules. In many cases, the slippage turned into outright cancellation, which is also costly (although often not as costly as the alternative of continuing to sink money into a project plagued by repeated delays). While the best companies reported that they cancelled only 10 percent of projects after starting full-scale development, the remaining companies cancelled 17 percent of all projects, or 70 percent more.

POOR PRODUCT DEFINITION IS THE SINGLE BIGGEST FACTOR IN PRODUCT FAILURE

While the factors influencing effective product development are highly variable, the study determined that the single biggest factor in the failure of products to meet market needs is poor product definition. Product definition, in turn, is linked directly to the ability of a company to discover and synthesize customer input. Although the best companies appeared to conduct more thorough, in-depth customer interviews and to visit customer sites for a longer period of time and with representation from more functions in the company than the rest, both groups spent, on average, only seven days at customer sites. This is particularly alarming when one considers that 70 percent of product life cycle costs are determined during the crucial product definition phase.

Unfortunately, companies often frame their market view and define product attributes to match the company's core competencies rather than to provide what the customer actually wants—and is willing to pay to receive. Companies often let internally driven product road maps or platform strategies drive fundamental business decisions (although it is possible to create a customer-centric road map or platform strategy). A study of "value innovation"[4] revealed that while 86 percent of new product launches were product line extensions, they generated just 62 percent of the total revenues and only 39 percent of the total profits. The remaining 14 percent of the new product launches generated 38 percent of revenues and 61 percent of total profits. The lesson? New products, not brand extensions, have the biggest impact on a company's bottom line. Examining customer requirements, thinking hard about how they are changing, and imagining alternative solutions increases the likelihood of generating totally new offerings that can command greater revenue and higher margins.

FUZZY THOUGHT, FUZZY DEVELOPMENT, FUZZY PRODUCTS

The incontrovertible evidence demonstrates that the logical focus and starting point must be the customer. Yet, as shown, half of the responding companies did not thoroughly understand the customer's needs before starting full-scale product development, and companies spent an average of only seven days on visits to customers' sites. Combined with the knowledge that the products producing the highest profits were new products, these facts offer a compelling argument for changing the product development process. But how?

The process of identifying customer value attributes for any product must be a disciplined one. This is often where the process starts to go wrong. Companies embark on the development process with few

tools, no metrics, and only a seat-of-the-pants plan for gathering, analyzing, and applying knowledge about what customers value. George Day,
in his study of Dupont,[5] found that:

> Each of the business teams were asked to make their own
> rank ordering of the attributes the customers are likely to use
> before the survey is made. Seldom is the internal list as de-
> tailed as the subsequent customer responses reveal. Normally
> about 15 attributes are found—whereas the management list
> is only 8 to 12 attributes deep. There is also wide variation in
> the rank orderings of the attributes within the business team.
> The sales force has one view, internal marketing another, and
> manufacturing and R&D managers very different opinions.

The lack of consensus among functional groups (sometimes referred to as silos) within an organization is often the misdirected starting
point for what has been described as the fuzzy front end of product
development. This fuzziness results from the lack of a cohesive definition of the customer value attributes in the product definition. Figure
1.1 illustrates this dichotomy. Often, the company's understanding of
the market is emotional or anecdotal rather than systematic, repeatable,
in-depth, and analytical.

A review of past product development projects, which PDC often
undertakes during its consulting assignments, can provide a useful
benchmark to understand a company's current product development
process. The process usually goes something like this: Someone or some
group in the organization gets an idea for a product and suggests that it
might be something customers would want. The idea may have been
generated from valid customer comments at a trade show, directly from
customer sales visits by a company executive, or from reactions to a
competitor's initiative, or it may emerge from the company's own
R&D efforts.

Once the company identifies the perceived opportunity, problem,
and technological innovation, it begins the development process. It
forms a team, creates schedules, assesses business risk and opportunity,
allocates money and resources, and begins development—often without

Figure 1.1. A product-centric approach results in fuzzy product definition, with varying views from different corporate functions. A customer-centric approach is cohesive, systematic, and repeatable, and is more likely to lead to one unified view.

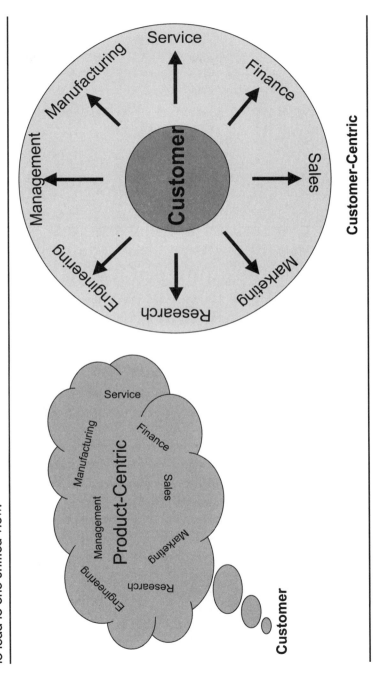

taking the time to poll the market in a systematic way in order to thoroughly understand the needs of the market and define the product attributes required to satisfy those needs. This is one reason why product development projects are delayed, over budget, misdirected, and, all too often, unsuccessful.

THE COMPANY DOESN'T ALWAYS KNOW BEST— AND THE CUSTOMER IS NOT ALWAYS RIGHT

Companies often claim, "We are leaders in our market, and we know what our customers' needs are," or variations on that theme. It is certainly true and obvious that many features must be included in a product. It is also true that managers in a company usually *do* know their market intimately and understand many of their customers' requirements. However, as the Dupont study revealed, it is *not* true that the company knows the relative value to the customer of the features incorporated in the product. Also, when product features are subjectively derived inside the organization, the development process does not identify *unexpressed* customer needs. Furthermore, potential customers often cannot or will not explicitly articulate their needs.

Robert A. Lutz, former president and vice chairman of Chrysler Corporation, in his book *Guts: The Seven Laws of Business That Made Chrysler the World's Hottest Car Company,*[6] postulated in his Law No. 1 that the customer is not always right. He cautions that customers don't always know what they want. If the process used in the product definition phase to determine customer requirements focuses only on *known* product features, you'll miss the *real* customer requirements that will delight the market. Lutz emphasizes that you can't expect your customers to do your creative work. "They want to be delighted, surprised, even challenged," Lutz comments. If you build only known features into your products, you are not differentiating your product from your competitors' products. This is like looking in the rearview mirror while you're driving. You'll have a great view of where you've been, but not of where you're going or, more importantly, of where your customers would like your organization to go.

Unfortunately, the mere process of gathering customer input can be seductive. It can lull companies into a false sense of security, into thinking that they have indeed done the research necessary to build products that will delight their customers. That's why it is so important to employ a discovery process that goes beyond most of the product development planning processes in use today.

Bio-Rad

Bio-Rad Laboratories, based in Hercules, California, is a multinational manufacturer and distributor of life science research products, clinical diagnostics, and analytical instrumentation. The company serves more than 70,000 research and industry customers worldwide and has approximately 2,500 employees. Founded in 1957, the company had 1999 revenues of approximately $500 million. Bio-Rad's Clinical Diagnostic Group was one of PDC's clients. Steve Binder, director of technology development, instituted PDC's MDPD process to define the critical features for instrumentation used to diagnose metabolic, genetic, infectious, and thyroid diseases.

Steve's team found that certain features were much less important to customers than the team had originally believed. For example, the team thought that the instrument's throughput (specimens per hour), a commonly used metric in the industry, was critical to a customer's buying decision. In fact, while throughput is a consideration, the MDPD process revealed that this characteristic falls far down on the list of desirable features and that greater throughput does not help sell the instrument.

This information told the design engineers that the throughput function in new instruments had to be competitive, nothing more. This affected a huge number of product-related issues: the time required to develop new instruments, the technological hurdles imposed on the instrument by higher throughput, the manufacturability, product reliability, maintenance service requirements, and most other elements in the product's life cycle—not to mention return on investment. Yet many groups in the organization automatically assumed that higher throughput was important and that maximizing throughput was a requirement for new products in this category. More throughput was considered the Holy Grail for new products by internal company functions, but not by the customers who would purchase the product.

The MDPD process helped Bio-Rad identify another significant yet latent need. One prospective customer who was interviewed expressed frustration that when the machine stopped in the middle of an extended test, with some test results completed and others incomplete, the machine would not release the completed test results until the problem was fixed. As simple as this sounds, consider the aggravation of completing 98 percent of a cycle of tests before the machine stopped and then being unable to get the results of the tests that had been completed. When Bio-Rad subsequently validated these findings with a broad survey, it learned that virtually all customers felt strongly about the ability to get partial results. Yet this feature was not incorporated into most of the competitive offerings on the market. The desire for this feature had not been stated expressly, but rather was uncovered during part of the MDPD process that involved analyzing the contextual environment of the laboratory. The MDPD process had revealed a significant customer need that was unmet by most of the current competitive products.

In defining product requirements, the MDPD process also separated fact from opinion. For example, the input from the team representative from sales was focused on the appearance of the unit, which this team member thought was significant. It turned out that while potential customers were concerned about the unit's footprint (how much desk space it required), they all agreed that appearance was not a critical issue. Their concern was functionality: Does it do the job?

Bio-Rad validated the information obtained during customer visits by surveying 400 customers around the world. Their customers' greatest concerns related to reliability and serviceability. It is not particularly surprising that these features were of primary concern, given the nature of the product. However, the MDPD process helped Bio-Rad clearly define and prioritize customer requirements and translate them into very clear and specific instructions to the engineering department regarding where to invest resources. In addition, the MDPD process focused the diffuse opinions among the functional departments and helped develop a unified consensus for defining and prioritizing customer and market requirements. This clearly optimized the product development process, eliminated unnecessary product changes, and reduced the time to market. The success of the MDPD process has led Bio-Rad to integrate it into the product development cycle on an international scale.

UNDERSTANDING THE VOICE OF THE CUSTOMER: PUTTING MDPD TO WORK

Truly understanding the voice of the customer is an essential starting point in the product development process. Yet this seemingly straightforward element of the product definition phase of the product development process is anything but straightforward. PDC's experience shows that companies often feel deeply and believe strongly that they know *exactly* what their customers need. These feelings and beliefs represent a psychological barrier that companies need to overcome before they can effectively implement a customer-centric product definition process like MDPD. *All* companies hold these beliefs. The universality of these beliefs, and the need to overcome them, is one of the motivating forces for this book.

To illustrate just how profoundly overcoming preconceived notions of customer needs can affect a company, consider the case of The Reynolds and Reynolds company, headquartered in Dayton, Ohio. Reynolds and Reynolds is the leading provider of integrated information management solutions to the automotive retailing marketplace. The company's services include a full range of retail and enterprise management systems, networking and support, e-business applications, web services, learning and consulting services, customer relationship management solutions, document management and leasing services. Revenues in 2000 exceeded $924 million, with approximately 5000 employees and a return on equity of 17.5 percent.

This well-run, successful company, delivering consistently solid fiscal performance, felt that its product definition process needed to be clearer, more systematic, and more repeatable. Reynolds and Reynolds suspected that its newly introduced products were slightly off the mark in terms of what customers wanted, and it knew that time to market was longer than desired. In addition, after introducing a new product, the company often had to expend considerable effort to change some product functionality and features.

Initially, the company considered a quality function deployment (QFD)[7] approach, but felt that such an approach would be cumbersome, time-consuming, and pervasive because it would involve wholesale business and cultural changes. It considered the MDPD process similar in principle to QFD, but smaller in scope and focused on the fuzzy front end, product definition. Moreover, MDPD achieved dramatic, documented results in the areas that most concerned Reynolds and Reynolds.

The first implementation of the MDPD process was a pilot project involving a new information system interface with a third-party vendor's software package. The MDPD process revealed that to meet customer requirements would require a change in the scope of the project. The product definition that Reynolds and Reynolds had initially envisioned differed significantly from the vision that emerged as a result of eliciting customer input through the MDPD process—a common experience. Reynolds and Reynolds realized that the investment necessary to meet customer requirements would be substantially higher than anticipated and the return would not be adequate.

The project was cancelled, but management was convinced that the MDPD process was a success. It had prevented a serious product development misstep and saved the company money. Being open to challenging internal assumptions about what customers wanted had enabled Reynolds and Reynolds to make a sound business decision based on the feedback from the MDPD process.

The second application of the MDPD process at Reynolds and

Reynolds had a very different outcome. This project involved improvements to an information system for managing car dealerships. Although customers had already voiced what they saw as the problems with an existing product, Dev Nanda, a product development leader, and his team decided to use the MDPD process. Reynolds and Reynolds management, and even some customers, were initially skeptical about the process, because they thought the product requirements had already been defined. "If we spent the time up front to get the proper definition, we believed, we would be able to move a lot faster in the development phase," Nanda says. "If you don't have the requirements completely defined, which is a premise of MDPD, you could go down a path throughout the development where you keep changing the requirements and end up spending more time and money. So, we went through the process. The total project from start to end was about ten months, and actually at the end of that, when we were through, the customers were really very delighted to see what we had done. I think that formed a foundation for moving forward with MDPD." MDPD is now part of the product development process at Reynolds and Reynolds on all critical projects.

Introducing MDPD

The MDPD process consists of four well-defined stages, each of which contributes to the ultimate goal of selecting a product or service solution for development. Typical product definition processes may include two or three activities before solution selection; MDPD encompasses fifteen, as shown in Figure 1.2. The process may seem burdensome to a team that is focused on getting a product out the door as quickly as possible. But companies that can muster the discipline to apply the process reap enormous rewards.

In Chapter 2, we'll begin to examine the planning stage of the MDPD process.

Figure 1.2. An overview of the MDPD process.

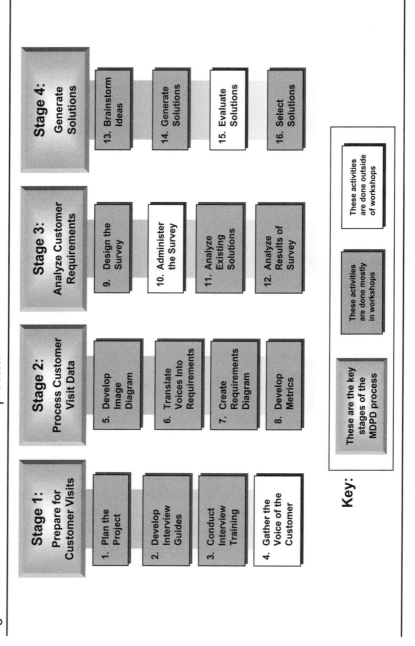

2

APPLYING THE TIMELESS SEVEN PS

Beginning at the Beginning

"Our plans miscarry because they have no aim. When a man does not know what harbor he is making for, no wind is the right wind."

—*Lucius Annaeus Seneca (4 B.C.–A.D. 65),*
Roman philosopher and statesman

"Failure to plan is planning to fail" is a very old cliché. General Sun Tzu, writing 2,500 years ago in *The Art of War*, observed, "The general who wins a battle makes many calculations in his temple before the battle is fought. The general who loses a battle makes but few calculations beforehand. Thus . . . I can foresee who is likely to win or lose." Many things have changed in the 2,500 years since, but the fundamental truth remains that without a well-organized and thoughtful plan, we may never achieve the results we expect or desire. That is why, as obvious as it may seem, Stage 1 of the MDPD process begins with the first of the seven Ps,[1] *planning the project.*

The planning process, step one of the first stage of MDPD, involves selecting the team, establishing a mission statement, creating a project plan, and developing a visit matrix. This chapter introduces these four elements of the planning process.

CRITICAL SUCCESS FACTORS AT THE PLANNING STAGE

Product Development Consulting has helped numerous clients in widely divergent industries, from Internet start-ups through *Fortune* 500 corporations, implement the MDPD process. Although the scope and complexity of implementation differs from client to client, many elements of the process are common across companies. Several critical success factors must be present in the planning phase of the MDPD process, regardless of the size of the organization, the scope of the project, or the industry. Two of these factors—the support of executive management and the support of the team project leader—are cited more often than any others by clients in postimplementation follow-up and appear to have the greatest influence on the success of the process.

The factors that must be present for a successful outcome are:

- *Management support*: Executive management must support, adequately fund, and empower the project team.
- *Cross-functional team*: Team members should represent all functional areas of the business involved in the product development project, and the composition of the team should achieve balance among the functional areas.
- *Project champion*: The team project leader needs to be a champion who is zealously dedicated to and supportive of the process.
- *Individual accountability*: Each team member should validate his or her individual accountabilities to the project.

We can't overemphasize the importance of the first factor: commitment of executive management. *Active* support by executive management is critical to the success of an MDPD implementation. Executive management must do more than pay lip service to the process. No matter how ingenious a product design methodology may be, or how dedicated the cross-functional teams, good intentions alone cannot engender success. Management must supply the resources that make in-depth customer research possible and must empower team members with the freedom and funds to conduct the research of which they are capable, at the level that customers deserve. Only then can organizations fully grasp the specifics of the customer's environment that provide the foundation for determining what customers want.

"The MDPD process really takes management commitment," says Denise Flinn, Internet testing product manager of Teradyne's Broadband Test Division, which implemented MDPD in its telecommunications division. "None of this would work without a strong marketing management commitment and division management commitment, because the process requires a cross-functional team on the front end to really make it work. It's gathering views from different perspectives in different disciplines, not just different people's views, that really makes the process work."

Senior Management Commitment Proves Vital at Dade Behring, Inc.

The experience of Dade International illustrates the importance of full and active management support *and* the commitment of necessary resources. Dade International, Inc. merged with Behring Diagnostics to become Dade Behring, Inc., a company with 2000 sales of $1.2 billion and 7,500 employees. Dade Behring, Inc. provides products and services for clinical diagnostic laboratories worldwide.

In 1997, the company recognized that a structured way to handle the front end—the often fuzzy area related to product definition—would improve its product development process. Senior clinical science associate Bill Naccarato observed, "We had become quite proficient at the development process from the stage *after* definition—what we call the feasibility stage—through commercialization. We were doing quite well; we had a process in place, and our development teams were familiar with it." The process was not sufficient, however. Dade Behring's process improvement manager, Roy Armstrong, concurred: "We had done benchmarking studies, and we knew we could get more bang for our R&D buck. Historically, we followed a sequential approach, where marketing told engineering what the marketplace needed and engineering translated that into product design."

Convinced that the company needed to restructure its front-end process, Naccarato and his colleagues proposed to the senior management group that oversaw product development that Dade Behring implement PDC's MDPD process. They won approval, funding, and critical management support.

They first applied MDPD to the development of a diagnostic analyzer that would facilitate workstation consolidation within hospital clinical laboratories. This analyzer would represent a significant expansion of Dade Behring's major product line. Although the diagnostic analyzer development project had already been underway for a few months, its leaders and the entire team admitted that they needed to do more to develop a shared vision of the product's goals. They recognized the importance of a shared vision in light of the fact that three-quarters of total life cycle costs are locked in by the time a company writes specifications and starts preproduction.[2] Thus, decisions made during the concept formulation and validation stages that precede full-scale development significantly affect total costs. The more successful a company's product definition process, the greater the long-term leverage. Product reliability and manufacturability have a large impact on ongoing costs; defining these characteristics into the product up front reduces costs going forward. Up-front work on designing for tests and doing simulations affects product quality and therefore cost. Most important, designing a product that meets the customer's needs reduces the beta-test rework and incremental releases that are necessary when the company gets the requirements wrong—especially when it misses a key must-have requirement.

In Dade Behring's case, the MDPD process helped to build objectivity into the design process (that is, looking at solving the problem from the *customer's* perspective), thereby reducing the risk of not meeting customer requirements and, in the process, bypassing the kind of infighting that tends to lead to costly delays.

Dade Behring's successful implementation of MDPD would not have been possible without full support from management. At one point in the project, two major players, the MDPD project manager from marketing and the engineering project leader, were skeptical about the value of the process. The marketing project manager was not convinced

that she should change her approach to gathering customer requirements (she thought she knew how to do it). The engineering project
leader had already conducted some customer research using Dade Behring's existing methods (pages of closed-ended questions, many about
potential solutions), was well along the path to a specific solution, and
didn't want to learn anything more. The general manager met with the
group, emphasized how important the MDPD project was, and explained why the team could not afford to take any chances on getting
this product wrong, even if it meant taking a little longer to get to
market.

At Dade Behring, support from upper management drove the project's momentum at a crucial time. At companies without such management dedication, MDPD projects have been derailed. This was what
happened at a large computer server manufacturer that was working on
implementing MDPD when the initial project sponsor was promoted.
The person who took the sponsor's place was unable to prevail in the
face of questioning by his manager, who had come from marketing and
believed that the company "already knew how to do this customer requirements gathering." The new sponsor chose not to continue the project. The project team members still thought the process was very
valuable but couldn't continue without management support.

THE IMPACT OF TEAM COMPOSITION ON PROJECT SUCCESS

Another critical element of the planning process is team selection, which
depends heavily on the scope of the project. For example, an MDPD
project for a product line extension will not require the same type of
team as a new product platform or an entire new product line. Whatever
the scope, however, teams must be cross-functional, including participants representing engineering, R&D, marketing, manufacturing, quality, service, and any other functions in the organization that are vital to
the product development process.

The optimal size for a team is about ten people, with five to seven key functional areas represented. Customer type, organization, culture, scope, past practices, and even politics determine the actual size of the project team. Schedules, availability, conflicts, cost, and complexity all become more difficult to manage when the size of the team increases. Even if they are not represented on the team, other parts of the organization can remain in the loop, since the MDPD process is designed to provide documented information for people who didn't actually participate.

Team Leadership Makes the Difference

The third critical factor in a successful implementation of MDPD is that the person who leads the MDPD effort be completely committed to the MDPD process. In some cases, the leader will be the project manager (or core team leader). In other cases, the inbound marketing person[3] will lead the team. Regardless of the team leader's background or titles, the key is that the team leader believes in the value of discovering customer requirements and is able to persuade reluctant team members that the process will yield valuable results.

The Role of Accountability of Individual Team Members

Each team member must be individually accountable. The individual team members must answer some questions:

- Why am I on this project team?
- Do I have the time available to do this properly, or do other job priorities take precedence?
- What depth of experience can I bring to this project?
- What effect will the success or failure of this project have on me, the department, and the company?

Planning Is Especially Important in Fast-Moving Industries

Effective planning is crucial for all companies, but for a start-up it can make the difference between survival and ruin. This is especially true for companies in the Internet arena, where cycle times have collapsed from years or months to weeks or days. Ironically, these may be just the companies that are tempted to bypass the planning stages in a misguided attempt to shortcut the development process and bring products to market more quickly. But new companies developing Web-based products don't usually get second chances. As David LaDuke, vice president of marketing for Linuxcare, a company that provides services for the Linux environments, put it, "You need a process like PDC has at the front end, because if you don't build the first offering in a way that attracts customers and gets them excited . . . then you won't ever get to that level where you can iterate and improve." As any baseball coach will attest, you can't score enough runs to win if you don't get anyone on the bases.

Linuxcare, launched in 1998, resisted the temptation to plunge headlong into development without planning. The company did not want to forge ahead into a venture, only to be forced to pull back, regroup, and begin again if customer response indicated that the initial offering had missed the mark. The product development group needed a focused direction so that it would know where—and where not—to devote its time and precious resources.

On the Linuxcare launching pad were a service-based Web site and plans to develop twenty-four-hour-a-day, seven-day-a-week telephone support augmented with onsite consulting for its clients. Although Linuxcare basically knew its target customers, it needed to present its services in a way that would reduce the perceived risk and enhance the benefits of using Linux. The company wanted to focus on partnering with the right software vendors, system integrators, and corporate enterprise users.

Moreover, the company needed to deal with the Linux guru

community—the independent experts who are not part of established organizations. LaDuke says, "Linux has been supported in
an ad hoc way over the Net, by people volunteering their own
time to help each other out. There's a lot of really expert people
out there who don't want to work in companies, but who have
incredibly valuable knowledge about Linux. Many maintain major
segments of the code." Obviously, to attract paying customers,
Linuxcare would have to provide service that was vastly superior,
not simply equivalent, to any existing solution, including the advice
of the Linux community.

A crucial part of developing an offering that would attract
paying customers was to form a crystal-clear—and deep—picture
of the challenges customers faced. As LaDuke said, "We have to
understand not only what customers are experiencing today, but
the latent, unmet needs that, when solved, are going to delight
them." LaDuke also knew that Linuxcare would need time and
commitment to achieve its goals.

Almost half the company was involved in the MDPD process.
The result was a road map charting the direction of Linuxcare's
offerings. "When we put together the system that would link Linuxcare corporate enterprises and Linux gurus together, what we
learned—we had an 'aha' moment—definitely had a big impact
on our forward-going development," LaDuke said. Based on the
information gathered during the process, Linuxcare also redesigned
its Web site. "We've also built it as a platform for delivering more
and more tools. But it was a total top-to-bottom redesign of our
Web site as a result of the research."

Without this process, Linuxcare would have gone to market
with the wrong product—a misstep that could potentially have
cost the company its life. "We thought we had the answer to what
customers really needed in online support," LaDuke said. "What
we found was that our assumptions did not match customer reali-
ties. We learned to view our own biases from the customers' perspective, and that made a huge difference in determining our
focus." The customer problems identified by the methodical
MDPD process enabled Linuxcare to understand its customers'
value proposition and identify things that the customers would not
have been able to articulate.

About the MDPD process, LaDuke says, "It's very involving. It takes a lot of commitment and time. But it's also, in the long run, a big timesaver." The commitment allowed the team at Linuxcare to compress the normal sixteen-week MDPD process into nine weeks to get the results they needed in the time frame they needed.

ESTABLISHING A MISSION STATEMENT

For companies itching to start development, the planning stages can seem superfluous. They are, in fact, anything but. The process begins in earnest with the development of the mission statement.

When a company decides to implement MDPD, it may, to use Seneca's seafaring metaphor quoted at the start of this chapter, have some idea of what harbor it is bound for. However, it must still determine the direction and speed of the wind, the conditions of the sea, the direction and duration of the tides and currents, and the exact course to its destination. In the corporate context, the answers to these questions form the basis of the mission statement. Too often, companies fail to give this in-depth analysis the attention it requires. Even if an organization has created a mission statement as part of the portfolio planning process, the analysis is worth repeating in the context of MDPD.

Developing a mission statement for an MDPD project provides the business context that helps to frame the approach properly and serves as the boundary or driver for the solution. Further, it helps align the expectations of team members and management and removes any ambiguity in the minds of team members regarding the purpose and scope of the project.

Carmen Najork of Becton-Dickinson comments on the importance of the mission statement to her organization: "I wouldn't start an MDPD project without very clear and engaging objectives that everyone understood and bought in on, so that when we were going through the process and when we finally finished we could say, 'Did we achieve those objectives?' I think that's the only way to judge a project."

The mission statement must answer the following questions:

- What is the company's motivation for this project?
- What are the *proposed* value propositions?
- What are the *proposed* main points of differentiation?

These questions and the answers to them must be part of the permanent project documentation.

Creating a Mission Statement

A team can work toward creating a mission statement by considering a few clarifying questions. First, what is the company's motivation for creat-

---

Components of the Mission Statement

Answers the Question:

"What kind of product were we charged with creating?"

Context

Overall summary of situation

Target Customers

Who they are
What their issues and expectations are regarding your product solutions or service
How they prefer to buy

Mission Description

Definition of what the opportunity is
Problem to be solved
Other information required to meet customer needs

ing the new product? Certainly, top-line P&L increases are desirable, but what are the reasons just below the surface? The answer to this question may describe, in abstract terms, the essence of the market opportunity. For example, an educational testing firm came up with the following statement of its goal, which also happened to define the market opportunity neatly: "There is a growing trend in higher education away from full four-year college programs toward the combination of two-year and four-year education. *Our goal is to define several product concept ideas that facilitate the transition of graduates of two-year institutions to four-year institutions.*"

Articulating Proposed Value

The team should consider the challenge of articulating the proposed value for the intended product or service. We say *proposed* since the product is not yet defined, but certainly the perceived market opportunity (which serves as the basis for the definition effort) must be justified, at least partially, by some type of value to the customer. Here again, the choice of words is specific and intentional: *Value* is defined as the product's functionality or performance per unit of cost to the customer.

The development of the value proposition must, quite obviously, address the issue of *who* perceives the value. For example, suppose a company proposes to develop a single cardiac catheter, capable of performing many routine cardiac catheterization procedures, to replace the several specific products currently required. Such a product would provide real, tangible value to a hospital's operating room buyer, who would no longer have to contend with the need to stock multiple unique products. Such a value analysis is extremely helpful to the team when it considers, in a downstream activity, whom to visit.

The experience of Bio-Rad Laboratories, described in Chapter 1, can help to clarify the intent of the value proposition. Bio-Rad, as you may recall, manufactures diagnostic instrumentation. Both Bio-Rad and the industry viewed throughput (specimens per hour) as the "holy grail" feature of diagnostic instruments. However, throughput was not the yardstick by which the target market evaluated new instruments, and thus customers would not have embraced a new instrument solely on the basis of higher throughput. The priority of this feature was low on the list of features the customers wanted in any new instrument. Customers wanted throughput to be competitive and comparable to that of other products on the market—nothing more. So, for Bio-Rad, spending product development resources to enhance throughput would not have had any payback. However, when Bio-Rad looked at the problem from the *customer's perspective,* the information it gained altered the *proposed* value proposition and resulted in a product that customers would actually purchase.

Think of the value proposition at this stage as a hypothesis to be tested during later stages of the process, rather than as a product feature or solution to be justified. The value proposition is designed to help the team focus on bringing the voice of the customer into the design process rather than maintaining a narrow product-out orientation.

The SWOT Analysis

A SWOT (strengths, weaknesses, opportunities, threats) analysis can provide valuable input to the mission statement. In a SWOT analysis, the main points of the product that may differentiate it from the competition are identified. The areas to be examined differ slightly for every business, but the following list can serve as a guide. The team should gather information regarding the current and probable future state of:

- The market conditions and trends
- Customer segments/target markets
- Current market position and position within segment
- Needs, dynamics, and requirements of the distribution channels
- Competitors and the competitive situation
- Technology analysis, trends, and discontinuities
- Environmental/regulatory conditions and expected trends

Assuming that competitive products offer a value proposition identical to the one the team has just articulated, determining points of differentiation also will help determine whether the team's functional representation is complete. For example, if the team proposed that its product would be differentiated from competitive products by low cost, then the team's roster must reflect this desire. The team must have adequate representation from manufacturing and engineering to ensure buy-in from those functional areas.

With data from the exploration of product differentiation in hand, the team can develop a SWOT analysis. Figure 2.1 lists the elements of a SWOT analysis.

Completing the SWOT analysis involves more than a cursory examination of the environment in which the business functions. A properly conducted SWOT analysis provides an objective evaluation that will help to identify the opportunity, frame the mission statement, drive the visit matrix, and lead to the development of the project plan.

The mission statement defines the opportunity and the problem to be solved. Armed with the information from the SWOT analysis, the team should be prepared to frame the mission statement. For example, the context of the opportunity might be that the aging boomer population is seeking more entertainment at home. Cable TV, DVD, Direct TV, and Internet technology are all rapidly expanding the availability of movies in the home. The target segment is the mass market of homes or apartments in North America with heads of household fifty years old

Figure 2.1. Elements of the SWOT analysis.

Strengths	**Weaknesses**
What are our strengths within the product line, brand, distribution, and other business model considerations?	What are our weaknesses and those of our competitors?
Opportunities	**Threats**
What opportunities do we see based on market size, industry trends, gaps in our product line, service, or distribution?	What threats do we face based on our weaknesses, our competitors' strengths, or changes in the marketplace or the technology?

or older. (The demographics can be broadly or narrowly defined.) The target market's preference is to buy online, but current solutions lack elegance. A possible mission statement might be: *To define and prioritize several new home theater system product concepts for (demographically defined) homes or apartments in North America, Europe, and Japan by June 20xx.*

DEVELOPING A PROJECT PLAN

The team's work activities going forward are designed as much to build acceptance, buy-in, and conviction as to discover delightful product functionality. Developing a schedule for the entire product definition project at this stage sets time investment expectations early in the program and allows individuals to clear their schedules for this important work.

International programs have longer time lines because of the need for translation and travel, so teams should allocate extra time if they plan international visits. Dates for activities that follow customer visits may change if the visits take longer than planned, but at least the team has a target. Developing the schedule also will uncover any deadlines external to the team that may drive the schedule, such as having products available for an annual trade show.

Figure 2.2 shows a typical project plan overview. The plan gives a range of times, but the project can realistically be accomplished in the shorter times. The critical element is that defining the product is the team's top priority.

DEVELOPING A VISIT MATRIX

The final planning step is developing a customer interview matrix. This step is so important—and so unlike the planning activities with which most team members will be familiar—that we will introduce the activity here and devote the whole of the next chapter to it.

Figure 2.2. A typical project plan overview.

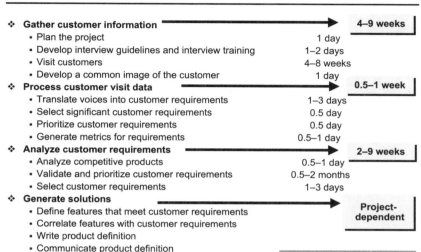

❖ **Gather customer information**	**4–9 weeks**
▪ Plan the project	1 day
▪ Develop interview guidelines and interview training	1–2 days
▪ Visit customers	4–8 weeks
▪ Develop a common image of the customer	1 day
❖ **Process customer visit data**	**0.5–1 week**
▪ Translate voices into customer requirements	1–3 days
▪ Select significant customer requirements	0.5 day
▪ Prioritize customer requirements	0.5 day
▪ Generate metrics for requirements	0.5–1 day
❖ **Analyze customer requirements**	**2–9 weeks**
▪ Analyze competitive products	0.5–1 day
▪ Validate and prioritize customer requirements	0.5–2 months
▪ Select customer requirements	1–3 days
❖ **Generate solutions**	**Project-dependent**
▪ Define features that meet customer requirements	
▪ Correlate features with customer requirements	
▪ Write product definition	
▪ Communicate product definition	
	TOTAL: 7–19 weeks

The customer interview matrix enables the team to visit the right customer segments and the right customers (users, influencers, and economic advisers) within those segments. The matrix does the following:

- Specifies key customer requirements segments
- Enumerates distinct segments (e.g., Europe, North America)
- Establishes market areas for distribution (geography)
- Ensures that a sufficient number of visits are planned for each distinct segment
- Identifies lead users (but doesn't focus on visiting them exclusively)
- Specifies key individuals who influence, purchase, or use the product
- Selects key customers to be visited (user, influencer, economic buyer, etc.)

Chapter 3 explores the details of planning customer visits, from deciding whom to visit to optimizing the number of visits.

3

THE CUSTOMER VISIT

Who Is the Customer?

"To solve a problem it is necessary to think. It is necessary to think even to decide what facts to collect."

—*Robert Maynard Hutchins*

TALKING TO THE RIGHT CUSTOMERS

Identifying the *right* customers to visit is a daunting task, yet it is the fundamental first step in successfully completing the MDPD process. Properly selecting the customers to visit is well worth the effort and will provide significant returns on the time invested. Simply visiting your largest, most important, or most profitable customers or concentrating on the largest volume segments will not give you a clear and deep understanding of product requirements. Using these criteria for customer visits can (and often does) lead you to present a skewed image to the product development team.

Consider what happens when a large, highly profitable customer requests that you incorporate a new product feature or new technology into your product. As a customer-centric company, you need to respond. But where will this lead? The customer may not yet have fully defined the problem that the requested product attribute is to solve. If you simply follow the path suggested by the customer, one of several things will happen. The product team may be unable to develop the requested

44

feature. Customer conditions may change, resulting in changed product specifications and delays or failure to deliver the product. Worst of all, your competition may identify the fundamental problem and propose and develop a solution while your product is still on the drawing board. Your competitor then grabs market share—including the same large, profitable customer that requested the solution from your development team in the first place.

Unfortunately, this nightmare occurs frequently and will continue to do so as long as companies search for solutions before identifying problems. Rushing into development as an immediate response to a customer request results in a product that may satisfy *some* of the product requirements for *some* customers, but may ignore or miss the requirements for a broader market or different clusters of customers. This failure to first identify problems is why developers often lament, "We surveyed our customers extensively prior to product introduction, yet the product did not achieve the market acceptance we anticipated."

SEGMENTING CUSTOMERS

The nature of the market opportunity serves as a guide to the boundaries for selecting appropriate customers to interview. This criterion is subtly different from traditional market segmentation standards.

For example, a manufacturer of home HVAC systems and thermostatic controls might divide its market into two broad segments, residential and commercial contractors. The residential segment could be further subdivided into developers of custom homes and developers of tract housing. The commercial building segment might be subcategorized into office, industrial, factory, and distribution building segments. The renovation construction market represents still another market slice. Or the manufacturer might choose to address the prefabricated home manufacturing market. These traditional market segmentation criteria are based on which end users buy the product and how.

While this method does ensure that all significant market segments are identified and included, it can quickly become unwieldy: The number of customer visits may grow untenably large when you add elements such as geography and customer size to the selection criteria.

Customer segmentation for the purposes of understanding the customer image must be based on different criteria. A more meaningful (and manageable) way for the HVAC manufacturer to segment its universe of existing or potential customers is to determine which of the traditional segments have uniquely *different uses* of the product. The *difference in the use* of the product or service by various groups of customers is the qualifying question when selecting customers to visit. This will determine whether or not to include a particular customer. Grouping customers on the basis of significant differences in the use for the product or service allows for the fact that customers in different geographical markets, at different points along the "food chain," or in different portions of traditional marketing segments may use the product in essentially the same way.

Becton Dickinson Vacutainer Systems (BDVS) took this approach when it implemented MDPD to identify customer requirements for blood sample collection products and services in the Asia-Pacific market. The team at BDVS began by segmenting the market geographically. Initially, the team suspected that significant differences in use existed among customers in the various countries—India, Malaysia, the Philippines, Taiwan, and Thailand—BDVS was targeting for product enhancements or new development. Considering the differences in culture, institutions, economies, demographics, and stages of development among these countries, this classification appeared reasonable. Local BDVS workers confirmed and reinforced the differences. Accordingly, the product definition team decided to investigate customer requirements and create an image of the customer for each of the countries represented.

BDVS created ten teams to select appropriate customers to visit in each targeted country, then developed and executed a plan to create five distinct images of the customer, one from each country. However, upon comparing the images of the laboratory functions and hospital staff for each country, the team discovered differences of use in only two areas. The significant customer images were similar enough to allow the team to focus on customer requirements for all the countries combined.

Use is the criterion for determining whether to include a separate segment in the customer visits: Is the use of the product in that segment significantly different from its use in other segments? Basing customer selection criteria on differences of use within a targeted market significantly reduces the set of customers to investigate. In the case of BDVS, when the team determined that significant differences in use did not exist among the various Asian countries, it was able to reduce the number of customer segments in the matrix considerably. It is important to note here that differences of use that are relevant to gathering customer data are not the same as differences of use regarding customer value. At this stage of the process, we are gathering only information on customer problems. Later in the process (see Chapter 10), we do statistical analysis to see if customers in different segments prioritize or value the requirements differently.

IT'S FAR FROM OBVIOUS

At first glance, unless there is a long distribution channel or numerous specifiers, influencers, or users, identifying markets or customers may appear straightforward. Beware, however, of not thinking hard about which customers to visit and identifying all the functions to include in the interviews—even when you think you know the customer. This often leads to disappointing sales results, costly product changes, or products that never reach the market or deliver their expected potential. Our experience with Dade-Behring, a major medical equipment manufacturer concentrating on chemical analyzers, illustrates the type of customer matrix you need to construct.

Dade-Behring's broad target markets were clearly defined:

- Hospitals with laboratory capabilities and with a certain number of beds, staff, and revenues
- Independent testing laboratories
- Research laboratories

Within those target market segments, the team identified the following key employees to interview as necessary to obtain a clear image of the customer: lab technicians, lab supervisors, doctors, nurses, administrators, research scientists, purchasers, and medical equipment distributors. Dade-Behring needed to examine the entire spectrum of customers for product usage, regardless of the complexity of the undertaking. The key to doing so in a manageable way is how the customer visit matrix is constructed.

In the Dade-Behring example, in each market segment, lab technicians and their supervisors are the end users of the chemical analyzers being considered for product development. Therefore, visits to lab technicians and their supervisors in each market segment should be included. These visits might reveal that customer requirements in a hospital laboratory were different from those in an independent testing laboratory, a research laboratory, or a pharmaceutical manufacturer. However, it is not necessary to include visits with doctors, nurses, hospital administrators, research scientists, purchasing agents, and medical equipment distributors in each segment. Three to five visits per function across all major segments is probably adequate to properly represent each function, since these functions are not directly affected by the product under consideration. The law of diminishing returns applies: It is unlikely that an increased number of visits to nonusers of the equipment would reveal any new concepts, problems, or opportunities.

Linear Bearings Manufacturer Discovers the *Real* Customer

While customer interviews must include all relevant consumers and functions in the supply chain, the end user must be the foundation of the customer visits. In the case of a leading international manufacturer of photographic film and printing equipment, identifying the right customer and understanding that customer's specific product requirements allowed the company to introduce what was at the time the most successful product in its history. Had the development engineers not looked beyond the R&D specifications to the real needs of the end user, the system might never have been developed.

The product being considered for development was a computer-controlled laser-based photolithography printing system that had originated in the company's R&D lab. This system was completely new and represented a substantial technological and productivity leap. Various subsystems (including computer software and hardware, laser technology, drive systems, and interface integration prototypes) were developed and tested separately from previous R&D work. Once the company proved the concept, it required a motion system using linear bearings for laser positioning of the film carriage.

Linear bearings (precision guideways that provide smooth and accurate rectilinear motion) have application whenever the desired motion is smooth, accurate, and repeatable to within microns (1 micron = 0.00040 inch). They are used extensively in the semiconductor industry, in the robotics and automation markets, and in medical equipment, packaging, photolithography, optics, vision, laser systems, automotive, and machine tools applications.

One application for linear bearings was the company's new printing system. Specifications called for the system, which was designed for four-color preprocessing of printing film, to be extremely accurate and to operate without lubrication. (Lubrication is necessary for most bearing systems.) The four-color printing process requires four individual films; for the company's new system, the dot matrices on the individual color film masks composing the image needed to be repeatable to 0.001 inch over an area the size of a newspaper page. If the images of the four individual masks were not consistent, the dot matrix color overlays would not be consistent and the final printed image would appear blurred.

The research designers developing the laser printing system were stressing accuracy and had developed an accuracy performance specification for the system. However, the performance specification exceeded the limits of the linear bearing mechanical technology—no manufacturer supplying linear bearings could meet the specification developed.

Perceptively, the bearing manufacturer looked deeper into the *end use* of the system and discovered an interesting fact: While the system did require high accuracy, the *repeatability* of the bearing system (an inherent characteristic of linear bearings), not its absolute accuracy, was the critical element. Translated into functionality, this meant that the optic component in the proposed laser photographic system had to travel to precisely the same position each time to deliver each laser dot on each of the four masks. The linear bearing system did this exceedingly well. In addition, the bearing manufacturer discovered that the printing system could tolerate a minuscule amount of dry lubrication.

Armed with the information obtained from visits with the printing equipment manufacturers' *customers*, the linear bearing engineers proposed an elegant solution that would satisfy the *end users* of the new printing system. The bearings were plated with a proprietary dry surface (originally developed for aircraft bearings) that exhibited lubricity under pressure, and which satisfied the system designers. The linear bearings provided the required repeatability without modification, and the printing system became the most successful new product introduced in corporate history.

CONSTRUCTING THE VISIT MATRIX

Creating a *visit matrix* is a useful technique for tracking targeted customer segments, customers, and functions. You need to involve all major customer segments. There is no hard and fast rule about which segments to include. When in doubt, sample a few segments to see if their problems differ across geographical locations, applications, cultures, or distribution channels.[1] Figure 3.1 shows a typical visit matrix.

The following is a guide to typical target values for a customer visit matrix:

- Ten to twenty customer sites total (may be more for multiple segments)
- Three to five individuals per site
- Three to five sites per market segment or customer type
- Three to five individuals per function or title

Consider visiting customers who use competitors' products as well as those who use yours. Visit happy, unhappy, and/or demanding cus-

Figure 3.1. Sample customer visit matrix.

Customer Sites	Traditional Market Segments and Nontraditional Customer Types						Functions / Titles					
	Sell Direct / Use Distributors	Never Customers / Were / Are	Lead Users / Average Users	Residential / Business	Variety of Products Used	Independent / Once Baby Bell	U.S. / Europe / Asia	Repair	Back Office	Super-visor	Recep-tionist	SUM
1	Direct	Never	Lead	Residential	ABC Co.	Baby Bell	U.S.	X		X		
2	Direct	Once	Average	Business	XYZ Co.	Baby Bell	U.S.	X				
3	Distributor	Are	Lead	Business	Ours	Independent	Germany		X			
4	Distributor	Are	Lead	Business	Ours	Independent	U.K.			X	X	
5	Direct	Were	Average	Residential	Ours	Independent	Japan				X	
Sum												

51

tomers, and also accounts you have lost. This should reveal the reasons you lost the customer in the first place and uncover needs your product did not meet in the past. Former customers may be reluctant to participate, fearing that your agenda is to resell them. You can overcome their reluctance by emphasizing that this visit is different: You are going to listen actively and base your product definition on a synthesis of the data collected.

Identifying specific customers to visit can cause significant delays as the team attempts to find appropriate individuals who meet the market segment criteria. The selection process will be easier if senior management has sent to the sales force specific instructions not only to cooperate but also to actively assist the team in selecting customers.

Working with your company's sales staff to create the visit matrix can require sensitivity and diplomacy on your part. Notifying the salesperson who oversees the customer account you intend to visit is always a good idea. Salespeople can be downright hostile if they are not informed, especially if the customer has complained about problems and has been ignored by product development teams in the past. (More on working with your company's sales staff in the next section.) If you sell through distributors, treat them like salespeople. Distributors also may be on your list of customers to visit, since they are part of the supply chain to your end user.

The visit matrix is intended to be a guide rather than a rigid mathematical prescription. The key factor is: If the segment represents a unique group that may have unique requirements, you should include it in the matrix. A typical matrix consists of approximately thirty individual customers.

Looking Beyond Today by Including Lead Users

Some interview teams should visit experts who may have insights into future trends. If there are experts in your field, visit them first so that your customer visit matrix and interview guide can reflect their insights into the future. This research differs from research into current users; this technology information will drive your solutions and help determine your customer visits.

Lead users have two distinguishing characteristics, according to Eric von Hippel, who has pioneered lead user research: (1) Their needs foreshadow the needs of the general market, and (2) they have sufficient incentive to try to develop solutions to their needs on their own.[2] Lead users often have needs that exceed the capabilities of existing products. Consequently, lead users have created their own patchwork products or commissioned a special product, which has allowed them to develop deeper insights into both the problem and attempts to solve the problem. Such insights are the reason to seek out lead users and learn from their experiences. For example, 3M was developing special sandpaper for curved edges such as those found on colonial furniture. The 3M development team chose to talk first with sculptors and with construction companies specializing in old home restoration—not because these individuals represented a market for the product, but because they already had experience in solving this problem and could provide insights into what the issues might be.

Because lead users foreshadow the general demand of the market, they should be part of the early visit schedule. They may not be customers, and they generally are not easy to identify. Asking the experts or academics in your field may help you find them. Figure 3.2 shows where lead users fit in the spectrum of users.

PREPARING THE VISITATION TEAM

We recommend that the visitation team consist of three people. A moderator and a note taker are essential; you can also include an observer. (Chapter 4 discusses the roles of each member of the team in detail.) Each team member should visit at least three customers to avoid getting a skewed view of customer issues. It is valuable if visitation teams stay together for all visits to build synergy for the interviewing process.

The Role of the Salesperson

Salespeople may want to contact the selected customers, but it is preferable either to have them make only an initial introductory call or

Figure 3.2. Schematic user profile.

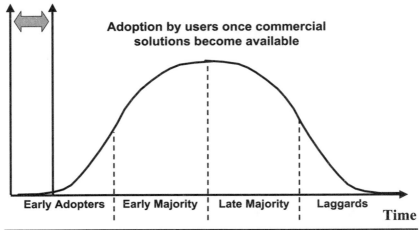

Source: Eric von Hippel, professor, Massachusetts Institute of Technology, Sloan School of Management, Cambridge, MA.

to have the visitation team members call the customer directly. If at all possible, the team should avoid having the salesperson accompany them to visit existing customers or prospects that the salesperson is cultivating. If the salesperson insists on attending, the team should talk candidly to her or him about the downside of having the salesperson there. First, the salesperson's presence may incorrectly send the signal that this is yet another sales meeting instead of an exploratory learning session to help product development. Second, the product definition team has had extensive in-depth training in how to collect customer thoughts. This training enables the team to leave the interview with a true feeling of what it is like to be a customer. Salespeople haven't been trained in this way and will tend to ask sales questions; their participation may lead the discussion in a different direction. Finally, your customers view the salespeople as their representatives for obtaining products in the near term and for obtaining support to resolve their immediate problems.

The customer interviews conducted as part of the MDPD process focus solely on understanding what it is like to be a customer or user of planned products and services. The objective is to let the customer talk at least 90 percent of the time and to obtain a word-for-word transcript of what the customer says. An intense focus on understanding the customer, rather than on selling, paid off for The Chinet Company. Chinet's MDPD project leaders drilled into team members the importance of differentiating themselves from the salespeople because they were visiting for a different purpose. As a result, a number of noncustomers said, "Well, if you guys care enough to do this much work and analysis, we'll at least give your product a try," and became customers.

While you don't want the sales team involved directly, salespeople and sales managers can be possessive and protective of what they see as "their" customers. To help make them part of the process without having them involved in the interviews, offer them the opportunity to read the transcript and even listen to the tapes. If a salesperson insists on attending, make a deal with him or her: The salesperson should be a silent observer, taking notes regarding what the interviewee says and observing the interviewee's body language. You also can share with the salespeople summary diagrams that give them a sense of the collective environment and of the customer requirements.

KNOWING WHEN ENOUGH IS ENOUGH

Figure 3.3 illustrates the principle of diminishing returns as it applies to how many customer sites you need to visit. The typical number of visits is between ten and twenty companies for each *distinct* market segment. The key to determining the right number of visits is to look at whether customers are repeating ideas or concepts you have already heard. You stop when you have covered your defined market segment and functions and you are not hearing anything new. If you have exhausted the planned visits and you are still hearing new things, you should schedule a few more visits within that segment.

RESEARCHING BREAKTHROUGH PRODUCTS

The MDPD process applies to the development of all kinds of products: incremental products, new products, and breakthrough products. Tech-

Figure 3.3. The number of new concepts becomes asymptotic after ten different site visits. The ideal number is between ten and twenty company visits for each distinct market segment.

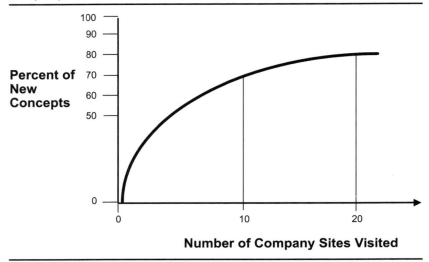

Source: Abbie Griffin and John R. Hauser, "The Voice of the Customer," *Sloan Working Paper no. 3449-92.* (Cambridge, October 1991).

nology push companies—those that develop new products by exploiting the fruits of internal research and development efforts—usually justify a product by saying, "There is nothing like this on the market." They may be right, but whether the market will embrace the new product depends on how well the innovation fulfills the market's need.

Look, for example, at the exploding and changing requirements in the personal communication market in the last 100 years. First, telegraph and telephone technology replaced the U.S. mail as the communication medium of choice. The introduction of the facsimile machine transformed telephone use. Cellular technology introduced telephone portability; the digital revolution introduced data communication; the Internet promises an information revolution; and broadband is changing everything. Yet each of these technology advances in the communications market was driven by the need to communicate and exchange information more quickly, clearly, securely, cheaply, and conveniently. The fundamental need has remained communication.

Moreover, this need can change with time. As breakthrough products become mainstream, customers look beyond the technology (how many shows can I tape at once with my VCR?) to usability (how easily can I program the VCR?). Carole Katz, director of market research and analysis at Avaya (previously Lucent Technologies) related her team's experience interviewing customers regarding a state-of-the-art video system.

> They're sitting at the table, and at the end of the room was the video terminal, video equipment, and next to the start button, on really large Post-Its—four inches by four inches—in big black, block letters written on the Post-It was the word "start" with an arrow pointing to the button. That image—you know, they didn't have to have a conversation with the customer around any of that. But when they brought that back and shared that with the team, everybody got it.

While the company that manufactured the product had been focusing on leading-edge features, the customer was focusing on how to use the product. This served as an important confirmation for Avaya in its product planning.

Much has been written about disruptive technologies, and a case can be made for technology push companies. But look more closely at the famous examples of products emerging from disruptive technologies, such as the Polaroid camera, Xerox copier, Sony Walkman, and Palm Pilot. They were breakthroughs because they *met the latent requirements of the customer before the customer became aware of the need*. If a company can identify those latent requirements, it can be first to market and enjoy a monopoly for a period of time.

Identifying and acting on customer requirements makes the difference. For example, the number of mobile phones sold annually increased tenfold between 1994 and 1999, exploding from 26 million to almost 300 million. Motorola was the world leader in the cellular telephone business until 1997, but it missed the shift in customer preference to the advantages provided with digital wireless technology by a year or two. In this short time, Nokia, previously a minor player in cellular technology, emerged to become the world's new leader.[3]

FAILURE TO PLAN IS PLANNING TO FAIL

Planning customer visits is the crucial first step in correctly identifying and understanding your customers' requirements. These activities typically take the largest amount of time in the project—often as much as 50 percent. This is time well invested, as the results of these activities will serve as the road map and validation criterion throughout the MDPD process. Unfortunately, these activities often defy easy characterization. They must be done right, but there is no one right way: Each organization's approach is unique. This also is an area that the project team, anxious to get on with the development project, often does not identify as the crucial first step. "A problem well stated is a problem half solved," according to Charles F. Kettering. And a project plan well developed is a project headed for success.

In Chapter 4, we explore the importance of the structured interview process in obtaining the true voice of your customer.

4

Understanding the Voice of the Customer

Hearing What Customers Are Really Saying

"The pure and simple truth is rarely pure and never simple."

—*Oscar Wilde.*

Ask, Don't Assume: The Need for Structure and Detail

So far, the MDPD process has not included direct customer feedback. At this point, team members who previously were going along with the program may begin to show signs of resistance. Some may question the need for such a detailed and structured process to gather customer information. Others may be convinced that they already have the answers. However, sticking with the process is more important than ever at this juncture.

The experience of a division of Honeywell was typical. The division had just introduced a successful new data communications product based on a new technology; the next step was determining where to direct the subsequent round of R&D spending. To select the best R&D investment strategy, a scaled MDPD effort was done to determine the immediate customer needs. Some members of the business team felt very strongly that a new device should include one particular set of features, but the results of the MDPD process clearly revealed that customers were much more interested in a different feature area. The confidence in the customer feedback from the MDPD work allowed the team to make trade-off decisions quickly. The next round of R&D funding was directed toward those products and features that customers wanted first.

Using a product-out orientation and not confirming the market-in requirements of the customer can have disastrous consequences. The not-invented-here syndrome, the arrogance that comes from creating a technological breakthrough, and a "we know what our customers want better than they do" attitude may begin to emerge. The result can be wasted dollars, wasted time, and the creation of products that bear no relationship to customer needs.

Too frequently, when companies attempt to understand what customers want, the interview process they use is solution-based or has a product-out orientation that seeks to justify an existing or proposed product or solution. Without a structured process for product definition, development teams, when faced with the need to define products, often proceed directly from hearing the voice of the customer to generating features or solutions, ignoring vital stages of the MDPD process, as shown in Figure 4.1.

Using a structured interview process reduces the risk that the product will not meet customer requirements. It leads to thoroughly defining customer requirements in repeatable, measurable terms, and it reduces the dependence on individual team members' knowledge and opinions. A structured process provides the necessary criteria to evaluate the ultimate product or service solution. Further, a structured interview process can lead to the discovery of customers' latent requirements or of "delighters" that can differentiate your product in the marketplace. Finally, if you can measure and fully understand an attribute, you can use it in competitive benchmarking and product positioning. By jumping directly to defining solutions before they thoroughly understand the customers' requirements and have validated those requirements in the broader market, development teams rob themselves of the understanding they need

Figure 4.1. In the rush to get products out the door, companies can be tempted to ignore several vital stages of the product definition process.

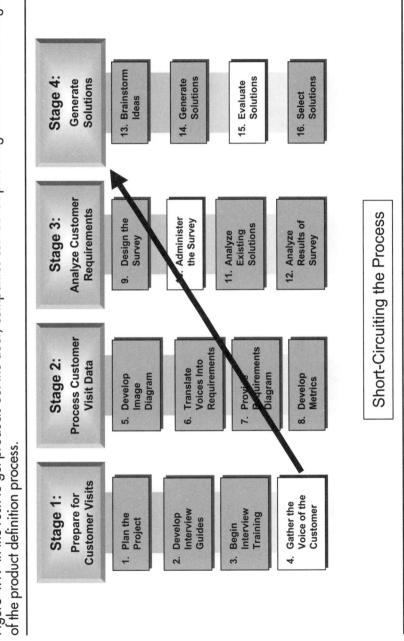

Short-Circuiting the Process

in order to evaluate those same requirements against present and future competition.

PICTURE PAINTING

The quality of the data gathered during customer interviews is paramount to successfully implementing the MDPD process. Moreover, obtaining information about the customers' expressed needs during customer visits is only the starting point in understanding your customers' true needs. Simply asking customers what they need is insufficient and often misleading, and can give you the false sense that you have actually heard the voice of the customer. Often, customers cannot articulate their true value-based needs. What they propose as a solution or product feature may or may not capture the opportunity they desire or solve their problems. In addition, gathering only solution-based information from the customer limits the solution set available to the development engineers.

Suppose, for example, that you are interviewing a customer about the requirements for the remote control device for an entertainment system. The customer complains that the remote is too small, so the development engineers begin to address a solution set that includes physical functions such as the size of the remote and the buttons. But the customer's true concern might be very different, such as pressing the wrong keys because of fat fingers or poor eyesight or even poor lighting. The buttons may even be too small because too many functions are included on the remote. If the team uncovers the customer's *real* problem by asking the customer probing questions in order to find the *root cause* of the problem, the engineer is free to address the *real* needs and to create value-based solutions to those needs. The design team may then consider options other than button size, such as voice activation, autoprogramming, various ergonomic designs, alternative technologies, or a combination of these and other possibilities.

DEVELOP THE ART OF PROBING

First-time users of the MDPD process face quite a challenge during interviews getting to the root cause of problems in order to understand the fundamental need. The number one shortcoming of interviewers is failure to *probe*. As noted previously, customers tend to talk in terms of specifications or features: "We need a 300-watt amplifier" or "The isolator must have a specific signal-to-noise ratio value." The purpose of the interview is to try to understand how features and specifications address a particular problem set. A specific signal-to-noise ratio for an isolator may indeed be a requirement, but knowing the end result that the customer hopes to achieve when given that ratio might lead to a different requirement—and a different solution.

While customers may lead researchers astray by suggesting solutions, customers *can* vividly describe their working environment, the problems they face, the objectives they are trying to achieve, or the difficulties they are experiencing with current products and solutions. The key is to probe for examples and details. The interviewer needs to find out why features or specifications are important and thoroughly draw out the customer's need. Some of the interviewer's most effective words and phrases are "Why?" "Could you explain?" and "Could you share an example?" Probing will help generate a vivid image of the customer's environment and real value-based needs. Questions such as "Is that a problem for you? Explain. What problem will that solve for you? Why?" may reveal latent or unstated needs that the customer cannot specifically articulate.

Asking questions to probe for information during an interview is like mining for gold. The interviewer is the miner and must probe to find the golden nugget. Asking a simple question gets you *expressed* data, which is like clearing the dirt away from the surface. You gather expressed data through active listening techniques. As you probe, digging deeper, you get more tacit data based upon facts. You are getting the rocks out of the way. Asking open-ended questions, getting the interviewee to tell you more, brings you to the fertile data of feelings and

Figure 4.2. Digging for gold in the interview process.

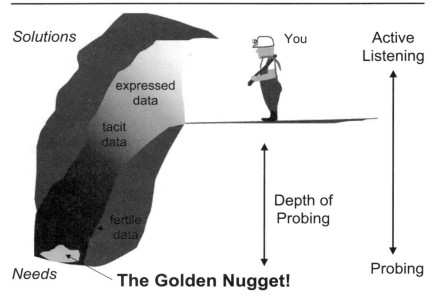

emotions. This type of data evokes a lasting image of the interviewee's situation and allows you to feel as if you are walking in the interviewee's shoes. At this point, you have unearthed the golden nugget, the small but very valuable piece of precious metal that every miner seeks.

Only deep probing can reveal the rich images that conjure up specific feelings and clear descriptions of the situation under consideration. Expressed data give you the other person's solution to a problem, but the golden nugget gives you the ability to address the other person's needs. Figure 4.2 graphically represents how deeply you need to dig for the data to ensure that the interview process thoroughly exposes customers' needs.

THE VALUE OF CONTEXT

In addition to asking many questions, exploring natural surroundings helps to foster a rich understanding of your customer's environment and is helpful in generating needs statements. Conducting the interview in the customer's environment reveals the contextual setting of the potential product's use and can give you significant insight into the customer's *real* needs.

A company that produces enterprise resource planning (ERP) software shared with us the value of the contextual setting for obtaining information about customers' true needs. During the interviews, the client observed the user of a competitive ERP system struggling to use the troubleshooting manuals that were part of the documentation. Although online and contextual help screens were readily available as part of the system, the complexity of the problem made it necessary to refer to the documentation. The manuals came in $2^1/_2$-inch binders, which, when opened, consumed most of the available desk space. And users required more than one manual to troubleshoot the problem. Consequently, the operators kept the manuals in their laps or on the floor, which was awkward, uncomfortable, and difficult. Customers did not expressly request changes to the manuals, but direct observation revealed to the interviewers that the current approach could be improved.

In subsequent interviews to validate this contextual requirement, other users confirmed that an improved documentation configuration was a significant element in the feature set for the new software. This led to a radically different approach to configuration of the manuals in later products, turning them from a difficult-to-use obstacle to a feature that delighted customers.

WORK IN THE CUSTOMER'S NATURAL HABITAT

When setting up the discussion guide for your customer visit, try to think as if you were the customer. Of course, this is easier said than done. When Dr. Dian Fossey wanted to study the mountain gorillas of the Virunga Mountains in Africa, she didn't visit a zoo that housed gorillas. She observed several gorilla families in their natural habitat to develop an in-depth understanding (a more 360-degree approach), allowing her to observe and vividly define the lifestyles of these gentle giants.[1]

Whether they are conscious of this or not, your customers' view of your product is all-encompassing and unconstrained. They perceive your product or service and your company in its totality, through the entire product consumption life cycle, from initial contact to order entry and through after-sales service and disposal. You view your customer through the preconceived constraints imposed by the very product or service you provide. You have to try hard to expand your sights to see your product as your customer does rather than myopically focusing your vision on one element of your product or service.

Our clients often ask us if they can conduct interviews with customers during trade shows or when customers come for home office visits. We recommend this course only when they have no other option and could not otherwise conduct the interview, since interviewing customers outside their natural habitats creates a limited view. For example, one of our clients decided to interview customers who were visiting company headquarters from South America. The product definition team had previously decided that South America was too far to visit considering the anticipated small market share. The risk of missing a requirement that was specific to South America was acceptable. The product definition team, rightly, took advantage of the visiting South American customers to explore their needs while they were at the home office.

CREATE AN INTERVIEW GUIDE, NOT A SCRIPT

Properly conducting a customer interview begins with the preparation of an interview guide. We use the word *guide* deliberately, as opposed to a script. A guide ensures that interviews consistently explore the major and important topics and should be a point of departure for insightful dialogue, not a questionnaire or market research survey.

Types of Questions for the Interview Guide

These are questions that are grounded in experience:

- "Describe the worst/best experience you've had with _____."
- "Describe the ideal product for _____."
- "If you were to purchase a _____ today, what would your considerations be?"

Questions should not be closed-ended, eliciting only a yes/no response. Good types of questions are:

- *What* questions focus on happenings: "What events led up to _____?"
- *How* questions focus on the way things happen: "How does the product allow you to ?"
- *Why* questions search for reasons: "Why is that?"
- *Could* questions are open-ended: "Could you conceive of an example of _____?"
- *What else?* will elicit more responses than "Is there anything else?"
- *Are, do,* or *can* often signifies a closed-ended question: "Are you satisfied with the product? Can you think of a case when?"

A long pause can be a question in itself and has several benefits. It gives the interviewee a chance to think, "What else can I say about that?" It also helps the interviewer by giving her time to think about whether a further probe is needed or about the next area to explore. Finally, a pause helps the note taker to review notes or take a breather.

WHAT THE INTERVIEW IS—AND IS NOT

The mission of the interview is to empathize with your customers. The means of accomplishing this is to actively listen and probe.

It is also important that you know what the interview is not. It is *not* a selling situation, nor is it intended to be an interrogation. If your questions imply in any way that you are marketing or selling, not listening to learn, you will lose credibility, turn off the customer, and gain very little insight into the customer's real issues. This is why we specifically advise against involving sales personnel. Including them in the visiting team creates the appearance of a sales call.

The interview is also *not* a validation of what you think your product's features should be. The role of the interviewer is to unearth new knowledge and to be extremely curious and inquisitive.

The Nitty-Gritty of the Interview Process

Interview Roles: Moderator, Observer, Note Taker

It is critical that you properly understand the input from the customer. That's why we recommend involving three people in each interview: the moderator, the observer, and the note taker. The role of the moderator is to lead the interview, build rapport with the customer, and probe to unearth value-based needs. The role of the observer is to watch the customer, soak up impressions, "listen between the lines," and support the moderator; the observer generally does not participate in the interview dialogue. The note taker is, as the term implies, a scribe. The more copious the note taking, the more customers feel that what they are saying is important to you and that you are actively listening.

If you want to tape the interview, ask for permission in advance, assure the customer of anonymity, and turn off the tape if it seems to be inhibiting the session. Taping the interview is not a complete substitute for note taking, however. Sometimes the tape is garbled and unclear. Often the tape stops and nobody notices it immediately, resulting in large gaps during the interview. Finally, when the tape is transcribed, technical terms may be lost, changed, or guessed at by the transcriber. If you use a tape, consider it the secondary source of interview data, with the primary source being copious note taking and active listening.

Tips and Tricks

Below are some generic interviewing tips and tricks. We include them only to emphasize the fact that the purpose of the interview is to obtain qualitative data and a rich, deep understanding of the customer, the customer's problems and needs, and the contextual setting within which the customer operates. Notice that the guide does not talk in terms of solutions—that is, product features or benefits—but attempts to uncover the customer's underlying needs and desires.

Introduction

The introduction should explain the purpose of the interview—for example, "We want to learn how we can improve the professional's fastening process for wood frame construction." It should emphasize that understanding your customers' problems and needs will influence future product development in your company. Your customers probably have met with other "factory representatives" in the past. They doubtless expect that this is simply another selling situation. It is *critical* that the interviewer alter that mind-set by *not engaging in any selling.* It is also valuable to mention that you may be asking some very basic questions to which your customer would expect you already have the answers. Explain that it is very important that you completely understand all aspects of the customers' needs from *their* perspective.

Bonding and Rapport

Asking the customer to explain his or her job or role in the organization is a good way to establish rapport and make the customer feel more comfortable. Establishing rapport is an important first step to a meaningful interview. While it may seem that spending precious limited time during the interview on this step is counter-productive, nothing could be further from the truth. A short dis-cussion on a topic in which the customer is obviously interested can quickly establish the necessary rapport. If the customer displays pictures, awards, or mementos, a simple question or comment may lighten the atmosphere and set the proper tone for the inter-view. People generally enjoy talking about themselves and should be encouraged to do so.

If the interviewee is brisk, formal, or "all business," bonding and rapport can occur on a nonverbal plane. One technique for accomplishing this is *mirroring*. If the customer speaks rapidly, the interviewer can quicken her pace slightly to an equal rate. If the customer makes body movements or postures, the interviewer can duplicate these movements. For example, if the customer leans back in his chair, the interviewer also leans back. (The natural tendency is to lean forward if the person you are talking to leans back; mirroring requires a conscious effort to do the opposite.) After a few simple gestures, your body language will promote a more relaxed atmosphere during the interview.

Questions to Elicit Customer Images

A good way to elicit customer experiences that provide vivid im-ages of the customer's environment or product use is to have them describe explicit examples of what they like or dislike about their jobs, and their best and worst days on the job. Have the customer describe the *ideal* way of doing his or her job: "If you had a magic wand and could change anything you wanted, what would your job be like?" Ask the customer to describe a quality product and why he or she would choose it. Ask about what changes the cus-tomer foresees in the future that will affect the job. Follow up each answer with a probe, such as, "And what problem would that solve?" Questions will vary depending on the function of the individual being interviewed and the customer segments being in-terviewed, but the essence of the interview guide is to elicit what it is like to be a customer.

A VIVID CUSTOMER IMAGE IS ULTIMATELY PRICELESS

An emerging technique in the world of consumer customer research is something called *storytelling*.[2] One method of employing this technique involves asking consumers to spend a few weeks thinking about how they would visually represent their experiences with a company. They are asked to clip magazine pictures (images) that express their feelings. The picture is a metaphor, which is the definition of one thing in terms of another, and can be used to represent thoughts that are implicit and unspoken.

Professor Gerald Zaltman from the Harvard Business School has developed a working metaphor laboratory and has used this technique to obtain insights from consumers concerning products about which customers feel strongly. Dupont, which supplies material to pantyhose manufacturers, looked to Zaltman to uncover an accurate picture of the feelings of women toward pantyhose. Probing into the emotions behind the images allowed Zaltman and Dupont to uncover women's true feelings toward pantyhose. One woman brought in a picture showing spilled ice cream, which represented how she felt when she noticed a run in her hose. Other images depicted a sleek Mercedes automobile, Queen Elizabeth, and beautiful women. Deeper probing revealed that pantyhose made women feel more sensual, sexier, and more attractive to men. Zaltman's research helped Dupont and pantyhose manufacturers to focus their development and marketing efforts on appealing to women's desire to feel sexy rather than their desire to achieve executive power. Companies have discovered that probing research such as storytelling elicits real-life stories from customers about how they behave and how they truly feel.

Another example of the use of imagery to uncover customers' true feelings is Kimberly-Clark, which attempted to reinvent the diaper business some years ago. The company knew that every time a kid graduated to underpants, Kimberly-Clark lost a customer for life. Meanwhile, parents were trying to help their children make the transition from diapers to underpants. The parents could express all the challenges and problems they faced, but they couldn't articulate the solution they needed.

A number of people at Kimberly-Clark had toyed with the idea of producing training pants. The transition product would look like underpants but would contain accidents in the same way a diaper does. Kimberly-Clark needed to discover if parents would buy this product. The company assigned a small team of employees to the task of probing customers to uncover the deep-seated emotions and challenges parents and toddlers face in toilet training. (Some of the team members were in the throes of training their own children.)

While visiting customers in their homes to uncover real-life stories, the team discovered some revealing facts. Stress in toilet training came from feelings of failure on the part of the parents, something that individuals in a focus group would never admit. During the storytelling process, team members discovered that the worst thing parents could be asked was, "Is your child still in diapers?" The team listened to embarrassing stories repeatedly and realized that parents viewed diapers as clothing that signified a particular stage of child development. Clothing had meaning, and the message that diapers sent to children and their parents was that the children were immature and the parents were failures.

In 1991, Kimberly-Clark introduced Huggies Pull-Ups training pants, a product based on customer storytelling and probing in-depth customer research. By the time the competition reacted, Kimberly-Clark was selling $400 million in Huggies Pull-Ups annually.

Another example is Intuit, the software company, which has institutionalized storytelling in its product development process with great success. Intuit Chairman Scott Cook said, "People don't buy technology. They buy products that improve their lives."[3] "Follow me home" is the name of one method of research the company uses. In this method, company engineers peer over customers' shoulders to better understand the use of the Intuit software. The process involves watching customers installing and using Intuit software in their homes. Visiting customers in their homes, Intuit engineers realized that the original releases of Quicken software took a sophisticated user a full day to install. This horrified the engineers. Intuit reacted quickly and simplified the installation process immensely. Storytelling and contextual observation of customers and noncustomers is now integral to product definition at Intuit.

Patagonia, the Ventura, California–based outdoor-sports apparel manufacturer, places customers' stories front and center in the company's product development and marketing efforts, with great success. These stories go beyond traditional testimonial advertising. The company uses feedback from customers and has even hired several of them to drive product improvement and new product development. For instance, several years ago, one Patagonia customer, Bob McDougall, a water sports expert, flipped his craft while negotiating some rapids in British Columbia. Everything in his boat, including his shoes, went down the river. After swimming to shore, he realized that he would have to climb from a canyon and hike several miles to his car—barefoot. He survived determined to design the ultimate climbing, hiking, and waterproof river shoe.[4]

CUSTOMER SATISFACTION SURVEY OR FOCUS GROUP IT IS NOT!

It should be apparent that finding out what the customer's *true* needs are is not as simple and straightforward as monitoring customer satisfaction surveys or conducting focus group interviews. Focus groups can be misleading or worse, and can point to inaccurate conclusions. Group dynamics influence the areas of discussion and customer opinions. The all-too-human desire for conformity coupled with aggressive or dominant personalities can distort true individual feelings within the group. It should also be apparent that obtaining a deep, rich image of the customer's needs will not only drive new product definition; it should provide a road map that, if followed, would result in the development of new products that can hit the sweet spot of those needs.

PREPARE, PRACTICE, REVIEW, REVISE, AND DEBRIEF

As mentioned earlier in this chapter, the number one shortcoming of interviews is the failure to probe. Another major shortcoming during the information-gathering phase is lack of preparation for the interviews. Thus, it is important for team members to practice their interviewing techniques and build their interviewing skills. In public speaking, great speeches rarely are extemporaneous; more often, they are diligently prepared, repeatedly rehearsed, and honed to perfection. Successful interviewing requires the same type of preparation. Johnny Bench, the legendary all-star catcher for the Cincinnati Reds, commented on the secret to his success: "It's practice, practice, practice."

Debriefing is as important as preparation, and it should take place as soon as practical after you complete the interview. Review your notes to fill in gaps and emphasize important comments while the interview is fresh, because no matter how attentive you were or how actively you listened during the interview, once the interview is completed, decay in recall from memory starts to occur immediately. The absolute necessity for transcripts, whether written or taped, should be obvious.

Successfully conducting customer visits and interviews will prepare the team to develop a *shared* image of the customer's challenges and environment as they relate to your company's areas of focus. Dawn Piacentino, program director of GRE programs at Educational Testing Service, says of the interview transcripts,

> I thought that taping the interviews was extremely valuable, because it wasn't someone going out, listening to someone, and then summarizing it in their own words, that may have their own little twists—we took the tapes and had them transcribed. So you had word for word. . . . Everyone got the same information and you could go back to those transcripts during the whole process and say okay, what did they really mean by this statement?

This will lead to the development of products that are consistent with and tap into the image you construct from the interviews.

POTENTIAL PITFALLS

The gathering of customer input from the interviews is the start of the implementation of the MDPD process. Keep in mind the garbage in/

garbage out principle: The process can only be as good as the information on which it is based.

Also, be cognizant of potential pitfalls to successful customer visits in and during the visitation program. One of these is the collapse of management support. The MDPD process may take several months, and project conditions may change over this period. Personnel, resources, and other variables in the project are dynamic and also can change. It should not be necessary—but it usually is—to reiterate that consistent management commitment to the MDPD process is required if the team is to conduct meaningful interviews. Management needs to provide the necessary human, financial, and schedule resources so that the team can successfully accomplish its mission. Giving the team the authority and the ongoing resources to execute the interview matrix and complete the interview process is essential.

While management interest and oversight should be visible and evident, intervention in or interruption of the process by management is not desirable. Once management has committed to the process, budget cutbacks, reallocation of resources, schedule changes, or doing more with less can cause havoc. Reaching your goal of gathering meaningful customer data is akin to taking a flight. The flight can be delayed, rescheduled, or aborted after takeoff—and if it is, you won't reach your destination. If conditions change and business considerations preempt a thorough implementation of the process, this is no different from a cancelled business trip—you still need to accomplish your business mission, but you may have to accept higher risk and less optimal conditions. You may need to replan the project in order to determine what you can and cannot accomplish. Any input from your customers is better than a product-out approach.

In Chapter 5 we will present techniques that allow the team to clarify, focus, synthesize, and prioritize the customer images. The *vital few process* method, *image diagramming*, and *language analysis* are some of the tools we will explore to sharpen the image of your customer.

5

SEEING LIFE THROUGH THE CUSTOMER'S EYES

Creating an Image Diagram

"If you get all the facts, your judgment can be right. If you don't get all the facts, it can't be right."

—Bernard M. Baruch

INVEST IN A PROCESS TO MINIMIZE FAILURE

By almost any definition, the rate of failure of new products is too high. Businesses that would not tolerate manufacturing error or defect rates of more than a few percent put up with a rate of new product failures that ranges from 35 to 80 percent. For example, historically, eight out of ten new products in the consumer market in the United States fail after introduction, according to Robert McMath, adjunct professor of marketing at Ithaca College, who is regarded as an authority on consumer product introductions.[1] In the manufacturing, commercial, and service areas, new product introductions also present a scene of carnage. Depending on what study you look at, between 35 and 40 percent of products introduced in these sectors also fail.[2]

The variables that determine the failure rate include whether the product is a consumable or a consumable durable, whether it is in the consumer or the industrial market, what time period is involved, and even the definition of failure itself. Although the experts and studies differ on the rate of new product failures, most business executives do agree that the failure rate for new products is much too high and the concomitant costs far too great.

While a company cannot avoid every product failure, most companies clearly would benefit considerably from a process that reduced the number of new product failures. That process begins with the company developing an image of its customers or potential customers in their environment. Some companies go to great lengths and considerable expense to understand the customers' environments, while others do nothing. Successfully identifying the image of the customer in the customer's environment allows the development team to conceive of products from the customer's perspective.

Often, companies do not have an established method for making trade-off decisions about competing consumer needs. As Buzz Sztukowski, vice president of commercial operations at bioMerieux, the eighth largest biological diagnostics company worldwide focusing on infectious diseases, puts it, "There has always been a struggle here regarding requirements. Engineering would have a listing of requirements that marketing would provide. And it would be difficult to say which ones are the most important, so how do I prioritize and make the trade-off?" With MDPD, when the design engineering team confronts choices and trade-offs in the design process, as it most assuredly will, the team's engineers will have specific criteria developed from the customer image and subsequent customer requirements to use in evaluating potential changes. Sztukowski continues, "What we've been able to do now is say, here are the requirements, here is how we would rank them, and then as we get through trade-offs between time to market, costs, and technical hurdles, we'll be able to make those trade-offs in a much more intelligent manner." The difference between companies that have a clear and vivid image of their customers and those that do not is reflected in the success rate of their respective new product introductions.

SOME COMPANIES GET IT, SOME DON'T

Have you ever heard the following complaints from members of a development team? "We surveyed our customers, and we still missed the mark with our product. . . . We know more about what our customers need than they do. . . . The customers keep changing their minds on us." These complaints and others like them most often come from product development teams that have not fashioned a product definition using a structured process to interpret the input from customer interviews. They have not probed below the surface to reveal the customers' true needs and have not understood the requirements from the perspective of the *customer*.

We specifically did not say that customers give us all their requirements. Customers may not know exactly what they want or need, which is why we extract images and use them to expand on what the customer says in order to *derive* requirements. Identifying images is the first step in deriving customer requirements based on customers' stated needs.

As we noted in the previous chapter, understanding precisely what your customers expressed during the interviewing process is key to developing an image of the customer's environment shared by the product development team.

WHY AN IMAGE?

You need only understand what happens when companies *don't* have a clear image of the customer to see the value in all this hard work. Many of the spectacularly unsuccessful products of the past can be traced to a distorted, incomplete, ignored, or misunderstood customer image. Consider the painful experience of the General Motors Corporation (GMC) with its introduction of the Cadillac Allanté in 1987. The Allanté was targeted to the younger luxury car buyers who were being lured by luxury foreign imports. Priced at $54,700, the Allanté was intended as a luxury car in a class with BMW and Mercedes Benz automobiles. The image of the luxury car buyer was intricately tied to the status of the automobile, which was perceived as high-quality, high-performance, distinctively styled, and reliable. The Allanté from GM did not match any of these images. The roof leaked, it lacked horsepower (at 170 hp), the body squeaked, and it fell far short of the quality and distinctive styling of its competition. The company had clear signs that the car was not ready for introduction, but it didn't make the hard choice to delay it; instead, it decided to launch the Allanté in spite of the bugs.

GM might have been successful with this approach if the automobile had been intended for the low-end, no frills, basic transportation market. But GM perpetuated the mismatch between the customer image and the product offering, trying to attract a high-end, quality-conscious, demanding buyer of luxury automobiles with a less-than-luxurious automobile. Consequently, the Allanté limped along for five years before GM pulled the plug.[3] Its annual sales never achieved half the projected volume.

Introducing a successful product requires a clear, concise, unambiguous image of the customer regardless of the target market, as other notable product failures demonstrate. The RCA videodisc didn't tape television shows; the IBM PCjr. had a slow microprocessor, was unattractively priced, and was introduced late; the NeXT computer used an optical drive that customers didn't want; New Coke offered a sweeter, "Pepsi-like" taste that consumers didn't want; Dry Beer was not understood or purchased; Divx played only a proprietary DVD format; *Time's TV-CABLE Week* required a customized edition for each cable system; and Polaroid's Polavision wet chemistry ran smack up against VHS videotape. Each was a world-class failure by a world-class company that ignored the fundamental customer image and customer requirements—at a combined cost of $1 billion.[4]

BUILDING THE IMAGE

Customers provide volumes of information during interviews. The voice of the customer contains statements about product-related features, benefits, attributes, problems, or wishes. While some of what customers say focuses more on their problems and needs, some statements evoke a sense of what it is like to walk in the customer's shoes. The latter is the image: a verbal, impressionistic characterization of the customer's environment. An image statement answers the questions "What is the customer's life like? What challenges the customer? What motivates the customer?"

Images come verbatim from the customer. They are distinct from statements concerning the customer's need for the product or for features of the product. An image should conjure up a concrete picture of the customer's surroundings. For example, the following are images selected from an in-house customer visit regarding a home theater system:

- *The components look like the lights of Tokyo stacked up next to the TV.*

- *There were three adults scurrying around the house frantically searching for the right remote control.*

- *It took me four hours and several phone calls to install the system, and then when I tried to show it off to my neighbors, it wouldn't work.*

The team's job is to sift through the myriad of statements contained in the transcripts to find statements that depict customer images. The transcripts probably will yield many more voices than images. The remaining voices in the transcripts represent the customers' views of their issues, missing product functionality, and sometimes suggested solutions. The following are more example statements from typical transcripts. Only the last is an image; the others reflect customer desires, suggested features, or solutions:

- *I want a system that fits in my suit pocket.* (statement of customer desire)

- *I'd like it to make all the adjustments automatically.* (customer has suggested a feature)

- *I would like it to weigh less than two pounds and easily fit in my briefcase.* (customer has suggested solution)

- *I have to get my reading glasses in order to read the numbers on the remote.* (image statement)

REDUCING IMAGES TO THE CRITICAL FEW

It is not unusual for the team to have extracted several hundred images from the transcripts. The goal is to reduce this to a manageable number of key images, which the team can then use to construct an *image diagram* (introduced in the next section). One of our clients, NASDAQ, started with more than 2,000 images culled from the transcripts obtained during visits to its customers, the NASD traders and financial institutions. In approximately half a day, the product team reduced this seemingly unwieldy number of images to thirty key ones that revealed major aspects of what it is like to be a NASDAQ customer. The product team at NASDAQ accomplished this not through magic but by applying a method that involves the team digesting labels and, by a process of elimination, collecting the most relevant key images.

This methodology is indispensable when it is necessary to reduce many things to a few. Using this method, the team can reach consensus regarding customers and their environment. By reducing the number of images to the vital few, the team can create a single document that tells the story of your customer and helps the team discover unstated requirements.

Selecting from hundreds of images the key twenty or thirty can feel like an overwhelming task. Team members often say, "We will miss some key images. There's no way we will ever get to twenty to thirty. I will feel uncomfortable with the results." Yet, after winnowing the images using the digestion method, these same people say, "Wow, we really did get to the vital few."

How is this done? The team goes through the process of image digestion. Team members read each image and select those images that they feel are the key images. There is no pressure to include or exclude any image. After everyone on the team who was involved in customer interviews has read every image once and selected those that they felt were key, we remove all the images that no one selected. As motivation, we count the images and show how many were removed. This gives team members an incentive to be more selective. Then everyone again

reads each of the remaining images and again chooses those that they
want to keep. Because there is no limit to the number of images one can
select for additional review, no one feels that he or she is missing anything when we remove images from active consideration. This process
continues. Ultimately, the goal is to select twenty to thirty images and
organize them into a format that facilitates deep understanding of what
it is like to be a customer.

CONSTRUCTING THE IMAGE DIAGRAM

With a manageable number of images extracted from the customer interviews, a team can construct an image diagram. Such a diagram describes, in concrete language, understandable to anyone, what it is like
to be a customer. If the team does not create and maintain a shared
image of the customer, preconceived perceptions or misconceptions
about the product and product use can cloud images and distort the
requirements derived from the interviews. "If we had bypassed the
image diagram, the team would never have understood our customers'
point of pain and to what level that pain needs to be alleviated if the
resulting product is to delight them," says Dev Nanda, a product development leader at Reynolds and Reynolds, an information management
company that serves customers in the automotive and document management markets.

Creating the image diagram is central to the process of fixing the
customer's current operating environment. An image diagram is essential for crafting requirements that have the customer foremost in mind.
Remember that the image diagram is intended to help the people inside
your company who are responsible for creating products understand
what it is like to be a customer. If these individuals did not interview
customers, they may not have firsthand knowledge of the customer's
environment and will be relying on the product definition team to clarify
exactly what the product should and shouldn't be. An image is the place
to start.

The image diagram organizes varied ideas and information. It provides a structure in which a diverse group can come to a common conclusion and in which every input is equal. It defuses emotion and minimizes confrontation while facilitating an open exchange of information. Teams should engage in discussion, not debate. Thus, the image defines the environment in which the product must function and provides the foundation for developing requirements. The image diagram must answer the question, "What scenes or images come to mind when you visualize your customer?" The language analysis (LA) method can be extremely helpful in answering this question.

Language Analysis Method

The language analysis method is a tool for organizing diverse observations and qualitative information into useful facts, for isolating problems, and for developing a greater understanding of those problems. The process is based on the KJ Method,[5] developed by Jiro Kawakita (Kawakita Institute, Tokyo, Japan) and modified to facilitate its use outside of Japan by Professor Shoji Shiba (University of Tsukuba and MIT).[6] The goal of the LA process is to answer an important question in a way that is organized, clear, and factual and that represents team consensus.

The process involves the following major steps:

1. Agree on the question to be answered. *The two important questions for which we use this tool are "What image or scenes come to mind when you visualize your customer's environment?" and "What are your customers' requirements?"*
2. Write and understand facts. *In the image diagram, these are the key voices of the customers that evoke a sense of what it is like to be a customer. In the requirements diagram (introduced in Chapter 6), these are the key customer requirements statements.*
3. Group similar facts to identify common threads.
4. Title the groups to create new shared concepts.
5. Arrange groups to show cause and effect.
6. Vote on the most important second-level issues and draw

conclusions. *We do not vote on the image diagram because all the images are equally important.*

7. Write the final summary statement that represents the overall theme and the answers to the question that is being asked.

Figure 5.1 is an example of an image diagram. The stratification, done from the bottom up, helps the team break free of preconceived structures and outlines. It provides new insight into needs by uncovering interrelationships and hierarchies.

In Chapter 6, we will discuss the translation of images into specific, actionable requirements in more detail.

Figure 5.1. Image diagram for a home theater system.

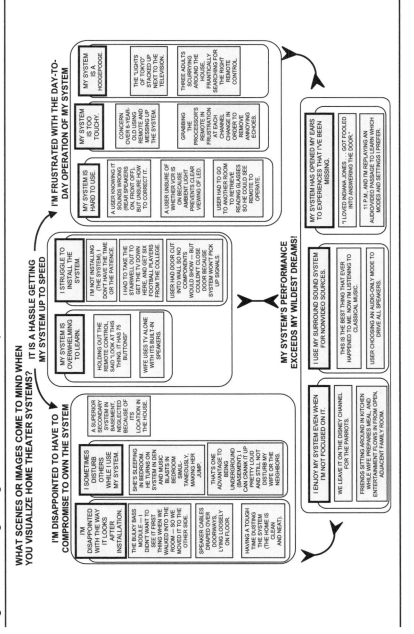

TRANSLATING THE VOICE OF THE CUSTOMER

Identifying Product Requirements

"Knowing is not enough; we must apply. Willing is not enough; we must do."

—*Johann von Goethe*

IMAGES + VOICES = REQUIREMENTS

At this point in the product definition process, the team should have a vivid picture of what life is like for the customer and a solid understanding of what irks the customer and what stands in the way of the customer getting his or her job done. Now the team must move from the specific to the general to define customer requirements—that is, what elements are essential to a product that attempts to solve the customer's problem? The process, illustrated in Figure 6.1, consists of linking a customer voice that identifies a need with the image of that customer's environment. From that linkage, the team can extract key words and identify customer requirements.

Denise Flinn, Internet testing product manager of Teradyne's Broadband Test Division, comments, "We were looking for a structured way to gather requirements because we were missing the up-front definition of what is the problem that the products we're trying to build solve. When we first started using the MDPD process, it actually took a

Figure 6.1. The process of translating the voice of the customer into requirements.

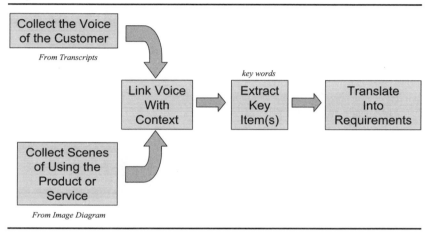

long time . . . because we were in a learning curve about what a requirement was. We had a completely different understanding of requirements. A requirement is a statement of a problem as opposed to 'the product must do this.' " A project team manager at a consumer goods company concurs: "A key insight from the MDPD process was focusing on the consumer's problems, not on the business brand or product form. This was a different and challenging way of thinking."

The translation step is where the rubber meets the road. It is partly an art form, because the team needs to extrapolate key ideas and to change or transform actual customer voices taken from the transcripts. Translation is one of the most difficult and challenging parts of MDPD; however, following the process described in this chapter helps turn what might otherwise seem a black art into something more predictable and repeatable.

CREATING REQUIREMENT STATEMENTS

Requirement statements are the essential elements and critical outputs of the process of listening to the voice of the customer, as Figure 6.2 illustrates.

Figure 6.2. Requirements translation overview.

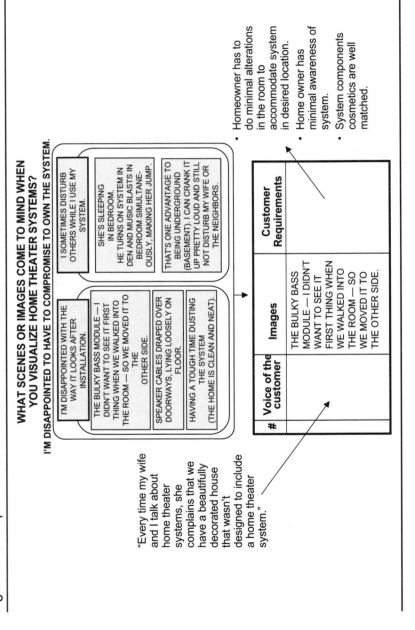

WHAT SCENES OR IMAGES COME TO MIND WHEN
YOU VISUALIZE HOME THEATER SYSTEMS?
I'M DISAPPOINTED TO HAVE TO COMPROMISE TO OWN THE SYSTEM.

"Every time my wife and I talk about home theater systems, she complains that we have a beautifully decorated house that wasn't designed to include a home theater system."

I'M DISAPPOINTED WITH THE WAY IT LOOKS AFTER INSTALLATION.

THE BULKY BASS MODULE — I DIDN'T WANT TO SEE IT FIRST THING WHEN WE WALKED INTO THE OTHER SIDE.

SPEAKER CABLES DRAPED OVER DOORWAYS, LYING LOOSELY ON FLOOR.

HAVING A TOUGH TIME DUSTING THE SYSTEM (THE HOME IS CLEAN AND NEAT).

I SOMETIMES DISTURB OTHERS WHILE I USE MY SYSTEM.

SHE'S SLEEPING IN BEDROOM. HE TURNS ON SYSTEM IN DEN AND MUSIC BLASTS IN BEDROOM SIMULTANE- OUSLY, MAKING HER JUMP.

THAT'S ONE ADVANTAGE TO BEING UNDERGROUND (BASEMENT). I CAN CRANK IT UP PRETTY LOUD AND STILL NOT DISTURB MY WIFE OR THE NEIGHBORS.

#	Voice of the customer	Images	Customer Requirements
		THE BULKY BASS MODULE — I DIDN'T WANT TO SEE IT FIRST THING WHEN WE WALKED INTO THE ROOM — SO WE MOVED IT TO THE OTHER SIDE.	

- Homeowner has to do minimal alterations in the room to accommodate system in desired location.
- Home owner has minimal awareness of system.
- System components cosmetics are well matched.

Chapter 5 discussed understanding the voice of the customer and generating images. To translate the voice of the customer into customer requirements, the team needs to pair the images generated with the customers' voices. The key is to identify requirements based on the pairing of images and voices.

It may seem rudimentary, but it's important to mention that requirement statements are made up of a subject, a verb, and a modifier. The subject is the user of the product—who or what desires a particular functionality. The verb identifies the missing functionality by answering the question, "What outcome do customers desire that they cannot now achieve?" The modifier states what is measurable or variable about this functionality. The modifier makes the requirement scalable, allowing the team to decide how well the requirement should be met after more data are available. (Chapter 8 discusses approaches to obtaining statistically significant data to support this type of decision making.) For example, in the requirement statement "Manager can provide reports in a maximum number of standard business application formats," the phrase "maximum number" modifies the requirement and identifies what is scalable or measurable about it. If the data show that this requirement is a low priority for customers, supporting one business application format might be enough. If it turns out to be a high priority, supporting a large number of formats—maybe even all the formats available—may be prudent.

The following requirement statements for a telephone software system at a remote call center, which include both good and poor examples, clarify this important step. The good statements present a required functionality and are quantifiable.

- "Data used by the call center should be entered by skilled administrative assistants." (Poor, because it specifies a solution: "skilled" assistants.)

- "Operator can input data with a minimum of keystrokes." (Good; fewer keystrokes is better.)

- "Operator can input data without making mistakes." (Poor, because it isn't scalable. Designing a solution to satisfy this requirement would mean that a developer couldn't stop until no mistakes were possible—no matter how significant or insignificant this requirement was to the customer.)

- "Operator can input data with minimal errors." (Good; fewer errors is better.)

Figure 6.3 provides a sample of a completed voice translation for your reference.

Frequently, teams are anxious to establish targets for the requirements, such as "A customer can obtain help in two minutes." Including a target restricts the requirement based on limited data, since we have not yet developed a statistical sampling of customers, nor have we yet assessed how well our competition accomplishes the function. We also might not want to preclude a solution that takes two minutes and five seconds. The reality is that the customer should be able to obtain help in a minimum amount of time. You should put off setting speed targets until you have statistical data on the importance of the requirement and an assessment of how well your competitors' solutions meet the requirement.

While the process of going through transcripts and translating customer voices into requirements may seem overwhelming, especially if you have interviewed eight individuals at five different customer sites, common themes will emerge after several transcripts. "We had a room designated to do this work and we practically filled the room with Post-Its

Figure 6.3. Moving from the voice of the customer to customer requirements.

#	Voice of the Customer	Images	Customer Requirements
1.	"I'd like to get to the person who is going to help me the most and the most quickly."	"I want an answer now: You hear that so many times, 'I got transferred six times.'" "There're still too many people frustrated by a non-human answering the telephone."	Customer obtains help quickly. Customer obtains help with minimum number of interventions.

Figure 6.4. What a customer requirement is NOT!

on the walls with various different voices and images," says Ken Reindel, formerly with Keithley Instruments. "We were just amazed at how much insight it gave us. But relatively quickly, within perhaps a matter of a day or two, we were able to distill it down. And, as we did, we began to see some product concepts miraculously emerging. We picked one of them and worked it further and developed it ultimately. To make a long story short, we developed it into a product that eventually turned out to be very successful. The result we achieved was not obvious considering where we were at the onset of the process."

SELECTING KEY REQUIREMENTS FOR REQUIREMENTS DIAGRAMS

Typically, the requirements expressed in the transcripts involve a broad spectrum of customer needs, which may number in the hundreds. This is more requirements than the team can digest. How does the team select the *key* requirements from among the many cited and balance these against the constraints imposed by the fundamental design, the time horizon, financial returns, market dynamics, technological hurdles, and other considerations?

We use the digestion method introduced in Chapter 5 to reduce the large number of customer requirements to the key twenty or thirty. Product definition teams tend to take this application of the digestion method more seriously than the previous application, since they are now removing requirements rather than customer images. But ultimately the method enables the team to arrive at the vital few requirements with confidence that nothing was left out.

Using the selected requirements, the team constructs a requirements diagram analogous to the image diagram described in Chapter 5. The requirements diagram expresses the team's understanding of the set of customer requirements, provides the key requirements for the product, and enables the team to share these requirements with their extended team and with management as appropriate. Figures 6.5 and 6.6 are examples of requirements diagrams.

The requirements diagram uses terms that are meaningful to both the company and the customer while providing direction to development. It focuses on a smaller set of the most important customer requirements. It creates consensus among team members, establishes the team's ranking of customer needs, and provides new insight into these needs, specific benefits, and development objectives by uncovering relationships and hierarchies among requirements.

The requirements diagram improves the efficiency of the product development cycle. Having a defined set of customer requirements against which to measure product development trade-offs results in fewer changes during the product development process and correspondingly reduces time to market. In addition, reducing the time to market reduces the cost of product development. This was the experience of Mike Grant, business development manager for The Chinet Company. After implementing the MDPD process, he said, "One of the things that would typically happen, before MDPD, is that in our product development process there would be a multitude of changes in design—either as we went through development or after we had rolled the product out. . . . With products that were defined with the MDPD process, the number of changes was reduced."

MULTIDIMENSIONAL REQUIREMENTS

When developing requirements, the team should consider *all* dimensions of the product consumption life cycle. Product definition teams tend to

Figure 6.5. Requirements diagram for a medical diagnostic system.

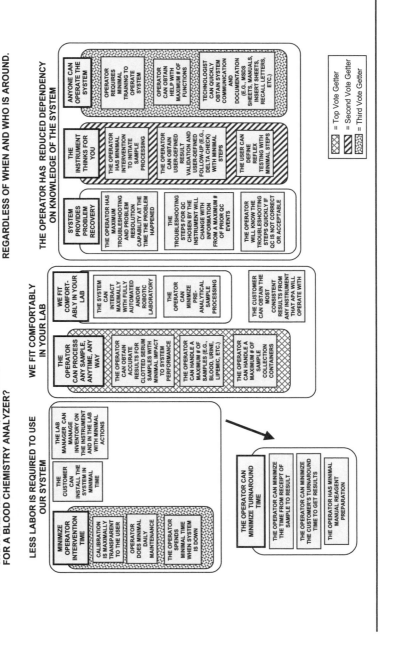

Figure 6.6. Requirements diagram for a home theater system.

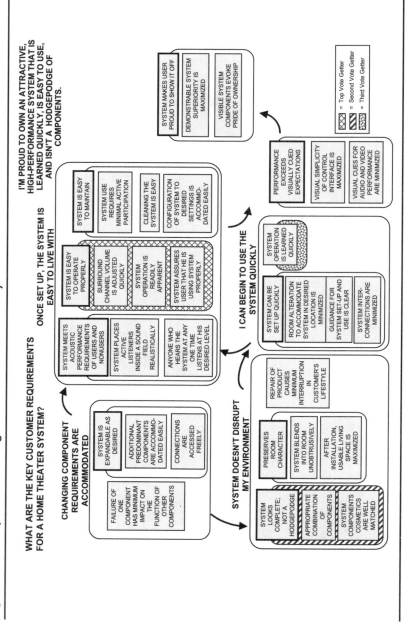

focus on customer requirements for the core product, a narrow concentration that may preempt inclusion of key requirements. The definition of success for a given development project confirms this tendency: Teams often measure success by the degree to which a product meets or conforms to the functional specification. The team needs to focus on the entire buying experience, not just the product's life cycle. Figure 6.7 graphically depicts the scope to keep in mind when developing requirements.

The Lexus division of Toyota Motor Company provides a good example of focusing on the entire buying experience. Today, most automobile manufacturers recognize and address the entire consumption life cycle. This was not the case when Toyota first introduced the Lexus in August 1989 and decided to separate the luxury car from the traditional Toyota brand and traditional distribution outlets by creating a new brand and unique showrooms. Lexus showrooms were not typical car warehouses; they were thickly carpeted, spacious, and well appointed, with upscale furnishings clustered in conversational areas throughout the showroom. The intent was to treat each customer as if he or she were a guest in someone's home. A salesperson greeted prospective clients professionally and courteously and offered refreshments. The salesperson then explored the client's background and desires and inquired how he or she could best be of service. The prospect was pampered throughout the sales cycle, during automobile delivery, and when the vehicle required routine maintenance or service. Loaner cars were routinely available. Some dealers offered a pick-up-and-deliver service.

This low-key, consultative approach differed markedly from the typical automobile shopping experience in the late 1980s. Toyota ap-

Figure 6.7. The scope of requirements should be broader than just product consumption.

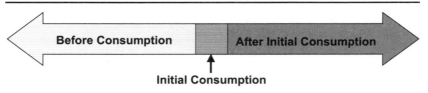

proached luxury car buying from a total consumption perspective, rather than using the "find 'em, fleece 'em, and forget 'em" approach that was common at the time. Clearly, Toyota understood the image of the customer it was attempting to attract to the Lexus and fine-tuned every aspect of the buying and ownership experience to appeal to that customer. The new luxury car was world-class in every respect, offering performance, safety, comfort, and styling, and Lexus offered levels of customer service that far exceeded the expectations of even the most demanding luxury car buyer. Contrast Toyota's approach in introducing the Lexus with GM's approach for the Cadillac Allanté, discussed in Chapter 5, and the importance of life-cycle consumption is evident.

Chapter 7 focuses on developing and assessing metrics to ensure that our requirements are unambiguous. We can then create a product definition that addresses key customer requirements, thereby eliminating the single largest cause of product failure.

7

ESTABLISHING METRICS

If You Can't Measure It, You Don't Understand It

"Facts do not cease to exist because they are ignored."

—Aldous Huxley

ESTABLISHING METRICS EARLY HELPS DEVELOPERS MAKE INTELLIGENT DECISIONS

Up to this point, the activities in the MDPD process have focused on trying to identify customer requirements for the product or service we are defining. Starting with customer interview transcripts, we isolated customer images and determined which of them were significant, created image diagrams, and translated the images and voices into customer requirements. Now, halfway through the MDPD process, we are ready to develop the metrics that we will use to test whether our product or service will satisfy the target market.

While the practice of developing metrics may be familiar, applying it to the product definition process often is not. Dev Nanda, a product development leader at Reynolds and Reynolds, comments that developing metrics can be "difficult and cumbersome, especially when you start to deal with each requirement and you can have multiple metrics for each requirement. You can have metrics that overlap requirements. . . .

Going through that, starting to get down to a meaningful few metrics which are helpful in terms of validating the requirements. . . . That's another area people struggle with."

MAKING REQUIREMENTS MEASURABLE

Armed with the customer image diagram, the customer requirements diagram, *and* metrics for each requirement, the developer can make intelligent decisions during every phase of product development. Yet teams often wait to test products with their target markets until they have developed a prototype, or at least a functional spec—at which point, resources have already been spent and it may be too late to make changes. This approach is fascinating in light of the fact that, based on PDC's experience, product development teams spend an average of one-quarter to one-third of their development cycle in testing stages. Many companies use a five-stage process for product development, with product definition accomplished in stages 1 and 2. implementation in stage 3, testing in stage 4, and production in stage 5. Companies typically develop metrics for the testing phase in parallel with the product development itself, usually during the latter part of the implementation phase—much later than the product definition stage. As they lay out circuit boards, develop software, or design mechanical components, developers make a constant stream of decisions that can't be completely anticipated during the design stage. When there are no metrics available and the product requirement specifications are ambiguous, the developer makes those decisions in the dark. Instead of waiting, we encourage teams to *test the requirements*. To do so, teams must develop relevant metrics.

Now let's look at what is involved in developing metrics for customer requirements. Figure 7.1 lists the activities or tasks completed in stage 1 of the MDPD process and the tasks to complete in stage 2. Knowing each requirement and testing it against soundly developed metrics assures us that we can measure how well our product or service will satisfy the customer requirements. A good metric provides a way to assess product performance during product design and development, prototype development, and beta test.

Figure 7.1. Developing and validating metrics.

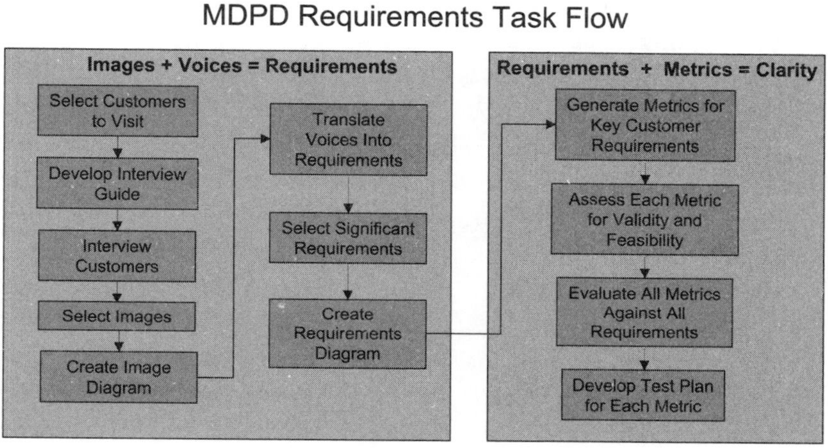

MDPD Requirements Task Flow

Images + Voices = Requirements

- Select Customers to Visit
- Develop Interview Guide
- Interview Customers
- Select Images
- Create Image Diagram

- Translate Voices Into Requirements
- Select Significant Requirements
- Create Requirements Diagram

Requirements + Metrics = Clarity

- Generate Metrics for Key Customer Requirements
- Assess Each Metric for Validity and Feasibility
- Evaluate All Metrics Against All Requirements
- Develop Test Plan for Each Metric

METRIC DEVELOPMENT

The purpose of developing metrics in the MDPD process is to provide a means of measuring whether the proposed solution does in fact satisfy the stated requirement.

A metric defines a way to measure *objectively* whether you have met the customer requirement. It begins with a verb associated with a quantitative activity (counting, measuring, calculating, scaling). For example, a metric for the customer requirement "minimize the effects of communication system problems on the user" might be: "Inject x *number* of errors in the hardware and software and run the desktop suite; measure the success rate." Or, if the customer requirement were to minimize downtime on a communications system, the metric would be mean time to recovery after a system failure. Minimization is still a subjective value, but you can scale the metric—i.e., change the value of what it measures—depending on the desirability of the requirement. (We'll talk more about weighting metrics on the basis of the importance of requirements in Chapter 8.)

The key here is that you have identified a metric that you can use to determine whether your product satisfies a customer requirement. This may appear straightforward, but when you actually get down to creating the metric, all sorts of gray areas and confusing issues can arise. For example, if a requirement is to minimize sample-processing time on a chemical analyzer in a hospital laboratory, when does the processing time that you are measuring begin and end? Do you measure from the moment a technician takes the specimen from the patient or from the moment when the specimen enters the system? Does the processing time end when the cycle finishes, when the report is generated, or when the doctor who ordered the test receives the results from the lab to assist in the diagnosis?

Keep in mind that each user will think of the requirement from his or her particular perspective. The lab technician, the supervisor, and the doctor will each interpret the requirement "minimize sample-processing time" differently. If the requirement were to minimize the time for the lab technician to operate the analyzer, the metric would measure the time for the analyzer to process a specimen. The supervisor, on the other hand, may be concerned with the equipment's total throughput. And, no matter how quickly a technician processed a specimen, the doctor would probably be dissatisfied if the system took a long time to deliver results. The metric in each case is time, but the critical factor is when the time period begins and ends. Therefore, an operational definition must be part of the metric.

MEASURING THE WRONG THING

Measuring requirements indirectly, measuring only one dimension, or misdirecting the focus of the metric can be worse than not measuring at all. A simple analogy illustrates this: Consider the case of a company that attempts to improve profitability, a critical metric for an enterprise. Management's goal (requirement) is to improve the bottom line. To achieve this, management decides to link sales compensation to company profitability by rewarding sales of more profitable products, reasoning that improved profits should follow. The metric seems sensible in theory, since the sales team will have an incentive to promote and sell more profitable products, presumably leading to bottom-line growth. Profits, however, are the result of a number of complex, interrelated business activities. The factors determining the profitability of the enterprise extend far beyond those under the direct control of the sales organization, which can influence only one element of profits: sales revenue or top-line growth.

You can imagine any number of situations resulting from this scenario. The enterprise can "profitably" lose market share and decline in size while increasing overhead expenses, ultimately forcing the restructuring of both the sales force and the entire enterprise. Or the sales force can achieve its sales goals while the company misses its profit goals; the sales team then becomes demoralized, and both the top line and the bottom line suffer. You get the picture. Since the sales organization can influence only revenue generation and top-line growth, it should be responsible for—and measured and compensated in relation to—these elements, not for something it cannot control.

In the same way, a product developer who focuses on the wrong metric can produce unintended results.

To be able to make trade-offs among requirements during development, product developers need metrics and targets for each requirement. Then the team can evaluate proposed solutions vis-à-vis their impact on each requirement. This subject is critical and worth one last example to firmly solidify the point. The case of a former PDC client shows the importance of developing the appropriate metric, determining its validity, and checking it against all customer requirements and potential solutions.

Norand manufactured wireless handheld computers for use in warehousing and inventory control. In 1994, Norand proposed the development of a handheld unit that would update a central computer processor in real time as inventory entered and left the warehouse. (Today, United Parcel Service, Federal Express, and many other transportation companies that need to track freight or packages and real-time inventory in transit use such systems.) Customer requirements centered on the weight, configuration, and functionality of the handheld unit. Weight was particularly critical, since operators used the system constantly and would handle the unit many times during an eight-hour shift. Battery life was also critical; the unit needed to operate continuously for at least four, and preferably eight, hours before requiring recharging or battery replacement. (Even today, the life of the most advanced battery system available for the latest notebook computer does not approach eight hours.)

The weight requirement was straightforward. The metric was primarily a function of the size and material composition of the battery. The proposed metric for battery life was total operating time, and also recharging time if operating time before recharging was less than eight hours. A battery that met the size and weight requirements had a usage time of approximately two-and-a-half hours, and thus required charging approximately every two hours.

The engineering department proposed using a fast-charge system to recharge the handheld computers during the warehouse employees' scheduled fifteen-minute relaxation breaks, which they took every two hours, and during the lunch break. Norand's R&D department had previously developed a fast-charge battery system for another program. Using a fast-charge system would allow the use of a small battery that would minimize the handheld unit's weight, while still providing adequate battery life. The fast-charge system would be costly, but the engineers thought that only one or two systems would be needed at each installation.

It wasn't until the development team visited the customers that the flaw in this solution surfaced. The metric measured the correct requirement, namely that the customer could use the unit for the maximum number of hours without recharging, but the proposed solution conflicted with the work pattern of the customer. Typically, an employee would check in at the beginning of a shift and would not return to the central check-in location until after the shift ended. The warehouses in which these systems would operate were enormous in size, with acres under one roof. If employees had to worry about recharging the handheld unit's battery, they would spend their entire relaxation or lunch break going to and from the recharging station. Clearly, this was an unacceptable solution, one that was proposed because the continuous use requirement did not reflect the totality of the customers' requirements. Ultimately, Norand addressed the linked issues of battery weight, life, and recharging capability by providing the handheld units with plug compatibility with electric personnel lift trucks, which were always within a few yards of the employee. Employees could then recharge the units easily during breaks or operate them in a plugged-in mode similar to notebook computers.

SMART Metrics

A good metric must be *specific, measurable, actionable, reasonable and timely*—SMART for short. Timeliness is particularly important. Teams often do not come up with useful metrics until after the product has been developed, believing that they can survey customers at that time to see if the product fills the need. By then, of course, it is too late to avoid wasting time and money developing the wrong solution. Metrics requiring input that you can't determine in advance don't help you evaluate whether a potential solution will meet customers' needs. Beware of cart-before-the-horse metrics, such as how easy it is to train people on the system.

You can use a single metric when the customer need is clear and unambiguous. Developing measurements for ambiguous requirements may be more difficult, since any one measurement will help you assess only part of the requirement. Take, for example, the requirement "unit must be comfortable to hold or operate." This requirement encompasses tactile considerations, weight, and ergonomic design. For requirements like this, you may need several metrics, or you may need to decompose the requirement into a set of less ambiguous or more concrete requirements that define each attribute, such as weight, separately and measure it appropriately.

Consider also the validity and feasibility of each metric suggested. Validity refers to whether the metric is measuring the right thing: We need to make sure that success in terms of a particular metric is indeed the outcome embodied in the requirement. The feasibility of a metric is relevant as well: If a metric requires an elaborate test simulator that costs a million dollars and takes six months to develop, consider measuring other attributes.

Usually the team can think of several metrics for each requirement. Figure 7.2 is a metric selection table for the requirement "I can quickly adjust the surround channel volume." This method of using symbols to tabulate feasibility and validity lends itself to cross-checking metrics against customer requirements in a subsequent step (Figure 7.3).

Once the team has completed all the metrics, you may find it valuable to construct a simple matrix to quickly match customer requirements to their associated metrics. Figure 7.3 is an example of this technique. This ensures that at least one highly correlated metric is associated with each requirement. The matrix also helps quickly identify customer requirements that are not addressed. You can eliminate those metrics that are not strongly coupled to requirements or that are redundant.

Once you have determined metrics for each requirement, develop a test plan to define explicitly how to measure against each metric. The plan (see Figure 7.4) is the "who, what, where, when, and how" of metrics. You need to determine:

Figure 7.2. Metric selection table.

Requirement: Surround channel volume is adjusted quickly.

Feasibility	Validity	Potential Measures
⊙	⊙	Count number of manipulations* to be in "surround sound" change volume mode
⊙	○	Measure time to change surround volume by 6 dB SPL
△	⊙	Calculate average time to change surround volume of uninitiated panel of users

*Button pushes, single or multiple buttons, cover or door openings, control interface reorientation of 90 percent or less in any Cartesian axis.

⊙ = High   ○ = Medium   △ = Low

Figure 7.3. The visual method of checking requirement coverage.

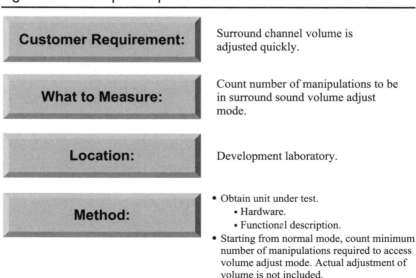

Figure 7.4. Example test plan.

Customer Requirement: Surround channel volume is adjusted quickly.

What to Measure: Count number of manipulations to be in surround sound volume adjust mode.

Location: Development laboratory.

Method:
- Obtain unit under test.
  - Hardware.
  - Functional description.
- Starting from normal mode, count minimum number of manipulations required to access volume adjust mode. Actual adjustment of volume is not included.

- *Who* is responsible for data collection
- *What* to measure and the accuracy (units of measure)
- *Where* and *when* you will collect measurements
- *How* you will collect the measurements
- *How* you want the results displayed

At this juncture, the team often wants to define a target for the metric. Generally, you should not set targets for metrics until you establish the priority of the metric, which you will do later in the MDPD process. However, if there is a major uncertainty about the magnitude or statistical significance of a measurement, or about what measurement is meaningful for customers, you can collect information on metrics when you survey the customers.

YOUR CUSTOMER, YOUR COMPETITION, AND YOU

A good metric specifies how to measure the satisfaction of your customers' requirements and maintains the consistency of the interpretation of the product definition throughout the development process. Developing metrics also establishes objective criteria for evaluating your proposed offering and your competitors' offerings against customer requirements. When evaluating how your proposed product and competitive products address customer requirements, you can identify areas that will differentiate your product from the competition. Doing so can be extremely useful for positioning your product in the market and will also supply factual information for developing marketing and sales promotional materials.

As we discussed in the sidebar in Chapter 1, Steve Binder of Bio-Rad had a significant experience with metrics and the MDPD process. Originally, the product definition team assumed that the industry standard for evaluating clinical diagnostic instruments was throughput (specimens per hour). In fact, the customers, although concerned with competitive throughput, clearly placed a higher priority on the release of completed test results in the event of system malfunction of the diagnostic instrument. This customer requirement—release of results—turned out to be significant for a broader group of customers than throughput. In addition, using the right metric proved vital in the evaluation of competitive products. Measuring release of results revealed that Bio-Rad had few competitors for this capability, and thus would enjoy a substantial competitive advantage for a feature that mattered greatly to customers.

In Chapter 8, we will explore market segment differences and the prioritization and selection of customer requirements to satisfy those differences.

PUTTING REQUIREMENTS TO THE TEST

Surveying to Validate and Prioritize Customer Needs

"The secret of business is knowing something that nobody else knows."

—*Aristotle Onassis*

THE NEED TO SURVEY

Like any solid structure, the MDPD process must rest on a strong foundation. The first two stages of the process created such a foundation by interviewing customers to collect information about their environment and requirements and then refining this information. We reviewed the construction of image diagrams that vividly bring to life what it is like to be a customer and the development of requirements based on information generated directly from the customer. Finally, we learned the importance of developing metrics to enable an objective assessment of whether our proposed solutions meet customer requirements.

It may seem that the team undertaking MDPD is more than ready to define a product at this point. But the team must complete one more stage before it is ready to generate solutions: It must validate, prioritize, and optimize the customer requirements it has developed. Because the team interviewed a relatively small sample of customers to derive these requirements, it needs to validate its interpretations and conclusions against a broader customer sample to generate a statistically significant set of data. Since there are rarely enough product development dollars to meet every customer requirement in an optimal way, the team must first prioritize the requirements.

Even if it were economically feasible to address every requirement, doing so is usually not necessary or even desirable. Different team members will place different priorities on each requirement depending on their perspective. For example, an R&D participant might place greater importance on requirements that address product performance, while a marketing participant might favor spending more on product-related services and packaging. Without clear priorities, the product developer or development team might view all requirement statements as equal.

The team can use survey techniques to analyze the risks and trade-offs involved in satisfying specific requirements or to understand how requirements differ from market segment to market segment. The results of the surveys provide information about which requirements the team can ignore with minimal risk and which can become the foundation for strong product differentiation. Using the survey techniques described in this chapter, a consumer goods manufacturer identified several customer requirements that the development team thought would be very important to solve. Surveys showed that although customers would be delighted to have the company's products address these requirements, they didn't consider the requirements very important. With this information in hand, the company was able to decide whether to spend valuable R&D dollars meeting these requirements.

Linuxcare, the provider of Linux services introduced in Chapter 2, provides another testament to the importance of surveying to validate and prioritize requirements. Says David LaDuke, vice president of marketing, "MDPD helped us focus. We actually did change one of our key projects . . . significantly based on the feedback we got from the survey process. And the process also reinforced some hunches we had about where we needed to go." Before surveying, the team had identified a bewildering array of requirements, all of which seemed to cry out for solutions. Surveys revealed that for several of these requirements, the current solutions in Linuxcare services were perfectly satisfactory. This allowed the team to focus all its energy on missing functionality and drove a reworking of the company's Web site. Surveying gave the Linuxcare team "a lot of really relevant learning about our Web site and the way we needed to provide Web-based services," LaDuke continues. "We've completely redesigned our Web site as a result. We've made it much more of a utility or a tool for customers to get support. And it's just the beginning. We've also built it as a platform for delivering more and more tools."

To find out which requirements really matter to customers, we use standard statistical tools in conjunction with the *self-stated importance (SSI)* survey, the *Kano survey*, and competitive analysis.

The SSI survey reveals how customers rank a given set of requirements on the basis of importance. This provides several checks on the interviewing and voice translation processes. The ranking validates that we have identified the requirements that really matter to customers. If a majority of customers consider a requirement unimportant, perhaps we have identified an insignificant requirement. The ranking establishes the relative importance or priority of the requirements for customers. Ranking also can help identify groups of respondents with similar qualities, demographics, or ways of using the product that you may want to segment. The Kano survey (discussed in detail later in the chapter) further clarifies segmentation for the proposed offering.

Ranking and segmenting the identified requirements may reveal new things about a market that no one knew before the survey, as Carole Katz, director of market research and analysis at Avaya, Inc. (formerly Lucent Technologies), discovered when she implemented Avaya's modified version of the MDPD process, referred to as Voice of the Customer (VOC), for a convergence project. Convergence refers to the combination of voice, data, and other functions in a single computer network or application. Initially, Avaya was focused on how to provide equipment and software that would address customers' convergence needs. Katz says, "We did a body of work and a very broad strategic study around convergence. The thing that bubbled up that was pretty revealing was that of the thirty-four priority requirements that we came up with, about two-thirds were requirements that really spoke to partner-ship and relationship as opposed to the product." The findings enabled Avaya to understand the importance of partnerships to the solutions it would develop.

Whether a project team hires an outside consultant or relies on internal staff, the steps involved in the SSI survey are similar to those for most traditional market research. They include:

1. *Establishing survey goals*
2. *Selecting customers and sample size*
3. *Determining methodology*
4. *Preparing the survey*
5. *Administering the survey*
6. *Analyzing the data*

MEETING SURVEY GOALS BY SELECTING THE RIGHT SAMPLE

The goals of the survey are straightforward: to validate and prioritize the customer requirements. The two main challenges in survey adminis-tration are obtaining good, representative lists and getting relatively high response rates.

The first challenge is ensuring the reliability of the survey lists. List brokers, magazines, direct mail companies, trade shows, and trade associations offer countless lists for sale. Other lists are available at no cost from a company's in-house marketing group, with names obtained from warranty cards, the sales force, the purchasing or service depart-ment, or prior direct mail campaigns. The list or lists you use should include respondents other than your customers, because using a list drawn only from your customer database may produce biased results.

A good way to ensure that you sample a cross section of market segments and functions is to go back to the customer matrix you devel-oped when you were selecting customers to visit (see Chapter 3). Figure 8.1 shows a sample portion of a typical customer matrix.

Figure 8.1. Sample customer matrix. The actual number of surveys required for each market segment and function will depend on the desired statistical significance of the survey.

Customer Sites	Traditional Market Segments and Nontraditional Customer Types							Functions / Titles			
	Sell Direct / Use Distributors	Never Customers / Were / Are	Lead Users / Average Users	Residential / Business	Variety of Products Used	Independent / Once Baby Bell	U.S. / Europe / Asia	Repair	Back Office	Super-visor	Recep-tionist
1	Direct	Never	Lead	Residential	ABC Co.	Baby Bell	U.S.	X		X	
2	Direct	Once	Average	Business	XYZ Co.	Baby Bell	U.S.	X			
3	Distributor	Are	Lead	Business	Ours	Independent	Germany		X		
4	Distributor	Are	Lead	Business	Ours	Independent	UK			X	X
5	Direct	Were	Average	Residential	Ours	Independent	Japan				X
Sum											
# for Survey											

ENSURING A GOOD RESPONSE

As mentioned, the second challenge in survey administration is ensuring the quality and quantity of survey responses. It is not unusual to have to repeat the survey or expand the sample size because responses are ambiguous, inconsistent, or misinterpreted, or because the number of responses does not constitute a statistically significant sample.

There are several ways to increase response rates. One way is to offer a gift or some other incentive for individuals or organizations to participate. Incentives correlate directly and positively with the number of responses. The rate of response appears to be proportional to the attractiveness, or value, of the incentive, i.e., the more valuable the incentive, the more people respond. Market Perspectives, Inc. (MPI), a full-service research firm offering online and on-site surveys as well as traditional paper and telephone research services, indicates that incentives are a major factor in determining the response rate.[1]

DETERMINING THE SURVEY METHODOLOGY

The delivery vehicle—direct mail, telephone, the Web, e-mail, fax, or in-person—you select for administering the survey and collecting data generally is a function of time, cost, market considerations, scope, and risk.

The emergence of the World Wide Web and e-mail has created new tools for conducting surveys. Conducting a survey electronically dramatically reduces response time; it is the fastest way to get machine-readable results. The disadvantages are that you have minimal control over responses and that obtaining quality e-mail lists can be difficult. Most businesspeople, your customers and prospects included, are being inundated with e-mail and have become very sensitive to spam. (It is not atypical for workers in high-tech industries to return from a one-week vacation to find several hundred e-mails in an electronic in-box and only a few pieces of physical mail on the desk.) Despite these drawbacks, online surveying is still the fastest method available for business-to-business research, assuming your customers and prospects are Internet users.

Figure 8.2. Relative interview costs.

Personal Interview	**2.5x–3.5x**
Telephone Interview	**1.5x–2.0x**
Mail Interview	**1.0x–1.5x**
Web or E-mail Interview	**1.0x**

An enormous amount of help and software is available for online survey sampling.[2]

Fax, telephone, and Web-based interviews offer the next fastest means of collecting survey data, with mail and personal interviewing being the slowest. With Web-based surveys, the responses go right into a database, removing the need for additional data entry. Costs vary depending on the size of the sample and the delivery vehicle used. Figure 8.2 shows the relative cost per interview, after initial setup costs, for each survey method. Web surveys, although they offer a low cost per response, require the highest setup charges—between $10,000 and $15,000 to develop and administer the survey and produce reports analyzing the results.[3]

There are also market considerations, such as:

- Does your market use e-mail regularly?
- Do your customers/prospective customers have fax machines?
- Do available lists include e-mail addresses and fax numbers? Professional organizations are just starting to add e-mail addresses to the information they collect from members, but this is not universal.

ELEMENTS OF THE SURVEY

In addition to a background/demographics section, the survey has two main elements. We use the first, the self-stated importance (SSI) portion, to determine how important each requirement is to the respondent. The second element, composed of a series of two-part paired questions, ascertains how a customer or prospect would feel if a certain capability existed or did not exist. This element is based on the Kano method of questioning, described more fully further on.

The background/demographics section of the survey provides basic information to help categorize respondent data. It asks for the respondent's business or industry, function, title or position, name, and e-mail address. The demographic section identifies the users and the decision makers. It validates segmentation decisions by showing whether different users rank requirements differently on the SSI and Kano sections. Differences that are not explained by demographics may indicate a separate market segment that was not previously identified. A sample of Section A, the background/demographics section, appears in Figure 8.3.

SELF-STATED IMPORTANCE OF THE REQUIREMENTS

Section B asks questions regarding the importance of each requirement. With these responses, we can determine the relative value of each requirement to our target customers, enabling us to choose intelligently how to allocate often-scarce development resources. Rankings range from "not at all important" to "extremely important."

One of the traditional problems with a self-stated importance survey is that respondents frequently rank too many things as extremely important. To reveal which of the extremely important requirements are most important, we suggest adding a forced ranking of these requirements. Stack ranking the requirements in the extremely important category forces the respondent to select the single most important requirements. Figure 8.4 shows a typical partially completed SSI survey with forced ranking.

The importance of forcing a ranking will be apparent when you analyze the SSI data and develop the reflected sum of the ranks (RSOR).[4] The relevant fact here is that the SSI survey report ranks each customer requirement in order of importance for the population being surveyed.

Figure 8.3. Typical survey questions to categorize survey participants.

What is the principal business of your company?

- Hardware development
- Software development
- E-business
- Combined hardware and e-business
- Nontechnology company
- Other: _____

What is your position / function?

- Software developer
- Help desk
- System administrator
- Architect
- Webmaster
- Web operations
- Other: _____

What department do you work for?

- Engineering
- Information technology
- Research
- Operations
- Other: _____

Figure 8.4. Forced ranking of the requirements. The respondent indicated that requirements 1 and 3 were extremely important, and therefore was required to further rank them using numbers.

Requirement How important would it be if	Not at All Important	Somewhat Important	Important	Very Important	Extremely Important	Ranking
1. You had more places to hold cups in your car?					✓	**2**
2. You could hold different size cups in your car?		✓				
3. You could access your drink in your car from several positions?					✓	**1**

The ranked requirements are compiled, summarized, and reported in graphical form. This immediately and clearly identifies the requirements that the customers being surveyed consider most important and least important. Figures 8.5 and 8.6 show samples of the completed reports.

APPLYING THE KANO METHOD OF QUESTIONING

Section C of the survey asks a series of two-part questions based on the Kano method of questioning developed by Dr. Noriaki Kano of Tokyo Riko University in Japan.[5] The two-part question is based on how respondents would feel if a certain capability existed or did not exist. The answers to the two-part questions will identify the requirement variables used to classify the need as *attractive, one-dimensional, must-be,* or *indifferent,* as discussed in the following section. An example of the Kano technique appears in Figure 8.7.

This questionnaire asks pairs of multiple-choice questions about user needs. Half of each pair of questions asks how you would feel if you had more of a particular capability than you have today; the other half of each pair asks how you would feel if you had less. The cup holder example demonstrates how one customer might answer such pairs of questions. Question 1a (more places to hold cups) asks how the customer would feel if a capability or feature is provided, and the customer's answer is marked with an X in the second column. Question 1b (fewer places to hold cups) asks how the customer would feel if a capability is somehow limited or absent, and the customer's answer is marked with an X in the last column. The second question, 2a, asks how the customer would feel if the cup holder could hold more sizes of cups than it can today; question 2b asks how the customer would feel if the options were limited.

The key to designing the two-part questions is that one half of the question is "functional" and the other "dysfunctional." One part is seen as positive: The feature is present; the other is negative or less positive: The feature is missing. In the cup holder example, the first question in each pair is functional: The respondent expects to have more places to

Figure 8.5. SSI graph. Note that the "very important" and "extremely important" rankings are combined to show the requirements that customers consider important.

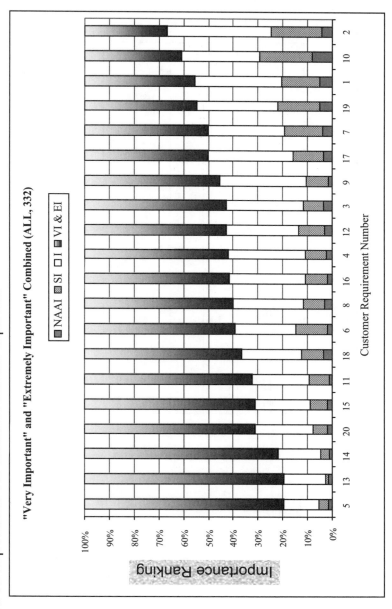

119

Figure 8.6. RSOR graph. Requirement number five is clearly the most important to customers.

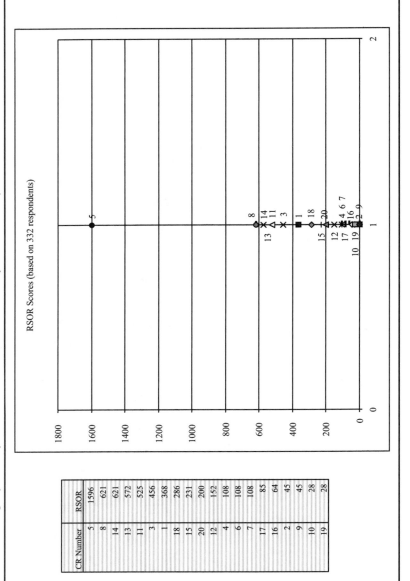

CR Number	RSOR
5	1596
8	621
14	621
13	572
11	525
3	456
1	368
18	286
15	231
20	200
12	152
4	108
6	108
7	108
17	85
16	64
2	45
9	45
10	28
19	28

Figure 8.7. Kano survey example.

How would you feel if	I would be delighted to find it that way (1)	I expect it to be that way (2)	I am neutral (3)	I would not like it that way but I can live with it that way (4)	It must not be that way (5)
1a. You had more places to hold cups in your car than you do today?		✓			
1b. You had fewer places to hold cups?	✓				✓
2a. You could hold more sizes of cups in your cup holders than you can today?					
2b. You could hold a more limited selection of cups than you can today?				✓	

Figure 8.8. Kano example.

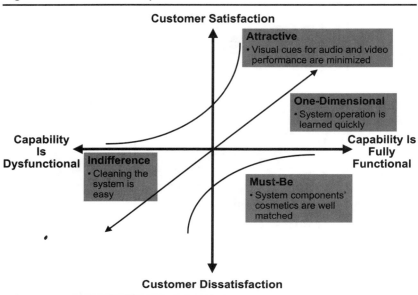

hold cups than today and would be delighted to be able to use more sizes of cups than today. The second question is dysfunctional: Holding fewer cups than today is not acceptable and the respondent would be disappointed if the selection of cup sizes were limited.

We can view customer requirements in two dimensions by plotting them on a graph with customer satisfaction on the vertical axis and the degree to which the attribute is functional or dysfunctional on the horizontal axis, as shown in Figure 8.8. Responses that fall above the X axis (the functionality line) indicate satisfaction; those that fall below indicate dissatisfaction. To the left of the Y axis, the capability is dysfunctional; to the right, it is functional.

ATTRACTIVE, MUST-BE, ONE-DIMENSIONAL, OR INDIFFERENT REQUIREMENTS

The Kano survey is a powerful took because it allows us to classify each requirement as attractive, one-dimensional, must-be, or indifferent.

When we know where a requirement falls, we know how much it matters to customers and how much of our development resources we ought to devote to addressing it.

Attractive requirements are those that satisfy or delight the customer. For example, "I can use my computer comfortably no matter where I'm sitting; I can see pictures on my monitor regardless of viewing angle." These requirements help shape a resultant product's value proposition. Customers are satisfied when the feature is present, and their satisfaction increases exponentially as functionality increases, i.e., small increases in functionality result in proportionately greater satisfaction. An example of this might be high-end speaker systems, such as Bose or Harmon Kardon, provided as standard car stereo equipment. Customers find this feature attractive because they did not expect it or ask for it. The presence of this feature adds to customers' driving enjoyment. However, few people would base a car-buying decision solely on the car stereo speaker system. Presumably, the customer is not dissatisfied when the feature—premium-quality audio speakers—is not present.

An attractive feature might differentiate your offering from competing models, but an attractive feature or attribute that is executed poorly results in dissatisfaction. For example, if the high-end speakers are sensitive to vibration or motion and require repeated service or even replacement, a significant level of dissatisfaction will occur.

Must-be requirements are basic requirements that the product *must* meet (e.g., "The car stops quickly in a maximum number of weather conditions; the keys on the data entry keyboard stick in a minimum number of conditions"). A must-be requirement is one that the customer considers essential. It might also originate from a regulatory agency or represent an industry standard. If your product lacks a must-be requirement, consumers will not buy it.

Some must-be items are not as obvious as industry standards. A good example is cup holders in automobiles. When cup holders first came out, they were an attractive feature. Until cup holders were introduced, consumers had solved the problem of how to drink coffee in the car by getting better cup lids or sticking some kind of add-on holder onto the dashboard. A car with a cup holder attracted customers and differentiated the car from those that did not offer cup holders. But after a short time, cup holders became a must-be requirement. Even Volvo, with its differentiating focus on safety features, was forced to add cup holders to its cars.

Just meeting must-be requirements is sufficient—you don't need to spend additional product development resources on fulfilling these requirements, since enhancing functionality will not improve product acceptance. However, *not* meeting them results in dissatisfaction. An auto buyer's satisfaction does not increase if a new vehicle is free of water leaks, squeaks, rattles, and wind noises, but dissatisfaction certainly occurs if any of these problems are present. If you fail to meet these requirements, you maximize downside risk without gaining anything, as General Motors discovered when it released the Allanté with a leaky roof, a squeaky body, and less-than-distinctive styling.

One-dimensional requirements are those that either increase or decrease customer satisfaction. The greater the functionality, the higher the customer satisfaction. The less the functionality, the lower the satisfaction. An example of a one-dimensional feature is automobile gas mileage. The higher the car's gas mileage, the better. Customer satisfaction falls in proportion to decreased product functionality—lower gas mileage. Returning to the cup holder example, soon after cup holders became a must-be, they became one-dimensional, at which point auto companies began boasting in advertisements about *how many* cup holders their cars or vans provided.

An *indifferent attribute* is a feature that the customers you surveyed do not value. Care should be taken to ensure that each segment feels indifferent about the same set of requirements. Differences in classifications can point to differences in use in specific segments. Identifying indifferent requirements can be extremely beneficial to the team when it is strategizing about features that add real customer satisfaction as opposed to those that may add cost but no measurable value.

It is certainly true that customer requirements change over time, as the cup holder example demonstrates. Attractive features tend to become must-be attributes as more products incorporate them and customers come to expect them. The same feature ultimately may become one-dimensional as companies try to boost the feature's appeal. The sequence also can go from attractive to one-dimensional to must-be. The cellular phone market is a good example of a rapidly changing environment in which requirements quickly morph from one type to another. In the past five years, digital technology has replaced analog as a must-have, and national and Internet access have become attractive requirements. Your challenge is to identify customer requirements while they are still attractive so that your product can have the marketing edge.

The Kano survey provides an objective criterion, from the customers' perspective, to guide the product developer in evaluating trade-offs among requirements, costs, development efforts, and time. With the metrics resulting from the survey, the developer can measure alternatives and handle challenges or delays in product development while staying focused on the customers' needs, rather than being swayed by internal pressures. This is exactly what Steve Binder, director of technology development at Bio-Rad Laboratories, meant when he said, "MDPD is a well-organized, believable, doable method that I could implement. The advantage is not only that I end up with the kind of information that I need, but that I have a process that is so thorough, so well documented, so well developed . . . that I could argue against any comer that I had done the job the right way."

Chapter 9 builds on the groundwork we have laid for creating the survey and presents the approaches to administer it.

BEGINNING PRODUCT COMMERCIALIZATION

Using Survey Results to Evaluate Existing Solutions

"I hear and I forget, I see and I remember, I do and I understand."

—*Confucius*

THE VALUE OF INTEGRATING PRODUCT COMMERCIALIZATION AND PRODUCT DEFINITION

Most companies consider product commercialization—the process of bringing a product to market—as a separate discipline from product development. During the 1990s, companies looked to improve the product *development* process, but usually brought their efforts only to the point at which the product shipped and manufacturing was able to produce it in high volumes. Today, more companies are looking for improvements in the new product *introduction* process. The difference in words is subtle, but it represents a major shift in focus and a recognition that product commercialization should be addressed early.

A company should formulate its product commercialization strategy during the product definition stage of development. Creating this strategy starts with the analysis of data from the surveys introduced in Chapter 8 combined with analysis of competitors' effectiveness in meeting market needs.

In trying to understand how to respond to the behavior of a market with a new product introduction, you examine such questions as:

- Is the market homogeneous? Does everyone behave in a similar way? Are particular patterns of behavior related to particular market segments? Are these patterns significant enough to demand separate analysis?

- Can you solve the market's problem regardless of any behavior patterns? Do you need separate solutions or options?

- How does the market currently deal with the missing functionality defined by the market requirements? Should you treat these existing solutions as competitors?

- What will your competitors be doing to improve their products? Are there industry or company trends that can help you make these predictions?

- How does the competitive landscape affect your product decisions? Do you need to be as good as or better than your competitors, or are you alone in your market?

This chapter will help you answer these important questions before they become impediments to success.

REFINING THE SURVEY DATA AND WEIGHTING RESULTS

The data from the self-stated importance (SSI) survey discussed in Chapter 8 revealed the requirements that customers identify as significant. The reflected sum of the ranks (RSOR) showed the relative importance of each requirement that they rated as "extremely important." The results of the Kano survey tested the value proposition inherent in each requirement. The results of these three tools can be used to assess the relative importance of each requirement for each market segment (if more than one exists), as well as to evaluate your existing product or service solutions and your competition's ability to satisfy those needs. Doing this requires more statistics and a commitment to some very detailed analysis of your survey results, but the outcome—a solution that delights your customers—is well worth the effort.

In Chapter 8, we simplified the examples and explanation of Kano surveying by assuming that everyone who took the survey scored each question the same way. In other words, all respondents found each requirement only attractive *or* one-dimensional *or* a must-be *or* indifferent. In the real world, different people place different values on each requirement. You may end up with 40 percent of respondents ranking a particular requirement as attractive, 30 percent ranking it as one-dimensional, 20 percent ranking it as must-be, and 10 percent ranking it as indifferent. The differences in ranking may be attributable to differences among markets, different perspectives based on the person's function or role in the organization, or simply personal preference.

Whatever the reason, you can't simply ignore the differences. Suppose you were in the desk manufacturing business and your research unearthed the following requirement: "The user wants a desk that is maximally resistant to damage." For customers in the education market, this requirement might be a must-be, while it might be merely attractive for customers in the commercial office market. (Office workers rarely subject furniture to the destructive forces that can be unleashed by school kids.) This difference is crucial to you as a product developer, since constructing a desk tough enough to meet the demands of the education market might cost so much that the desk would be priced out of reach of the office market.

As the desk example shows, we need a mechanism for combining individual customer rankings to determine how to evaluate each requirement in light of different market segments and different uses of the product. The concept evolves around the satisfaction/dissatisfaction scale created from responses to the Kano questions introduced in Chapter 8. (Remember that the results of the Kano questioning determine whether a respondent considers the requirement attractive, must-be, one-dimensional, or indifferent.)

In Figure 9.1, we have identified the area above the functionality line as the customer satisfaction plane; the attractive and one-dimensional results are combined to create a "better than best-in-class" category. Another way of saying this is to say that the customer wants a solution that is better than the current solution or approach to fulfilling the need. *How much* better depends on the mix of attractive and one-dimensional requirements: the more attractive, the higher the level of satisfaction if you fulfill the need. The area below the functionality line is the customer dissatisfaction plane, in which we combine the must-be and one-dimensional results to create a "worse than best-in-class" category (the customer is dissatisfied). Responses falling in this plane indicate that the customer would not be satisfied if the new solution was worse than what is available today. An extreme case would be *all* respondents saying that a requirement is a must-be and that the solution must be

Figure 9.1. Kano chart with satisfaction and dissatisfaction planes.

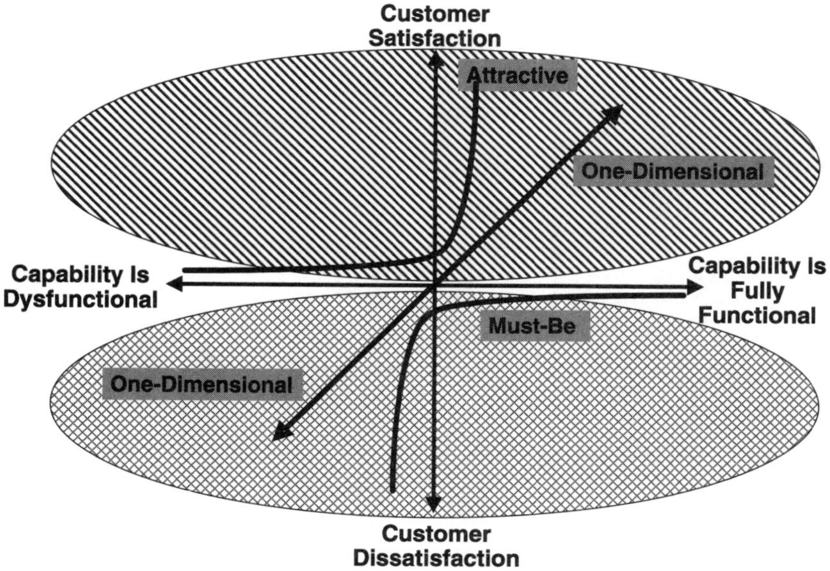

better than it is today. A less extreme case would be a mixture of one-dimensional and must-be responses, so that the respondents' degree of dissatisfaction with a solution worse than what is available today is not high, but does exist.

By plotting each survey response on the table shown in Figure 9.2, we can convert the Kano results into weighting factors. Later, these weighting factors will help the team clarify choices and make trade-offs among customer requirements. Since the relationship between functionality and satisfaction is nonlinear, we need two weighting factors for each requirement. We derive one weighting factor by combining the percentage of responses from the if-better-than (IBT) values and the other weighting factor by combining if-worse-than (IWT) values, as shown in Figure 9.2.

Once we calculate IBT and IWT values for each of the require-

Figure 9.2. IWT and IBT weighting factors come from combining the percentages of responses to paired questions in the Kano survey.

	% Response by Category					
	Must-Be	One-Dimensional	Attractive	Indifferent	Reversed	Questionable
12a. If an instrument will interact with fully automated laboratory and/or robotic systems, how will you feel? 12b. If an instrument will not interact with fully automated laboratory and/or robotic systems, how will you feel?	26 **45** (IWT)	19	21 **40** (IBT)	32	0	2
13a. If an operator does not need to centrifuge samples before putting them on an instrument, how will you feel? 13b. If an operator must centrifuge samples before putting them on an instrument, how will you feel?	8 **11** (IWT)	3	62 **65** (IBT)	23	0	4
15a. If an instrument actively notifies an operator of QC failures, how will you feel? 15b. If an instrument has no active QC failure notification, how will you feel?	57 **78** (IWT)	21	10 **31** (IBT)	9	1	2

ments, we map the values to the Kano satisfaction/dissatisfaction factors for each customer responding to the survey. Figure 9.3 shows the four quadrants to which the IBT and IWT values will map. By observing where a requirement falls, you can determine whether the requirement is strong or weak. Each quadrant conveys a distinctive meaning. Being closer to a particular corner indicates a stronger requirement. Proximity to the center of the square indicates a mix of segments or respondents, mixed responses, or a relatively weak feeling about the requirement.

Figure 9.4 is an example of Kano mapping from the real results of a survey conducted by a medical diagnostic company. As you can see,

Figure 9.3. Kano satisfaction factors. At the origin, both IBT and IWT are zero—i.e., no one answered the question with a valid response.

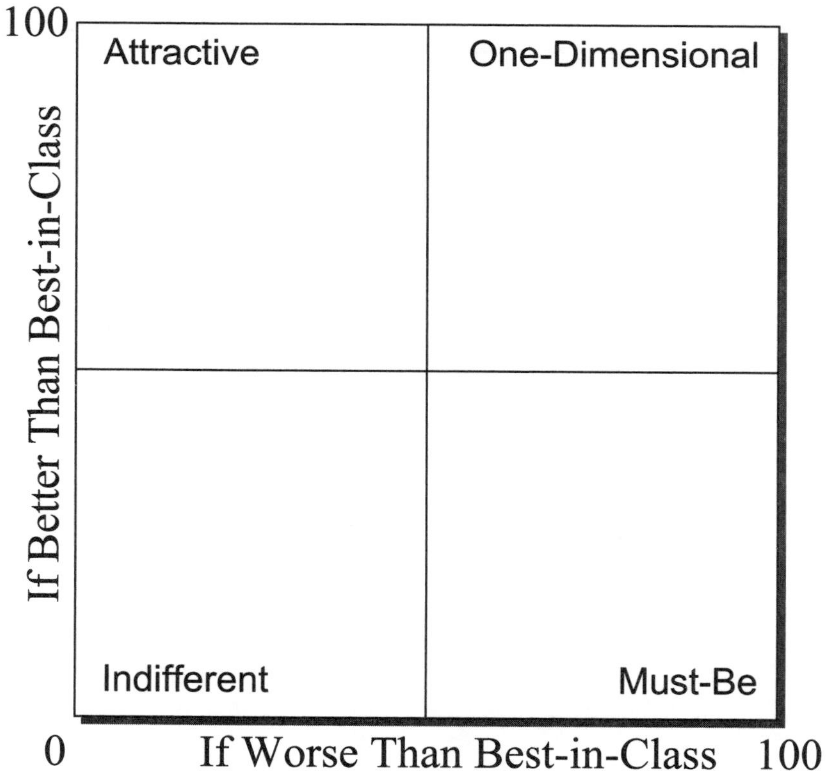

Attractive	One-Dimensional
Indifferent	Must-Be

If Better Than Best-in-Class

100   0   If Worse Than Best-in-Class   100

Figure 9.4. Kano plot with requirements and IBT and IWT scores.

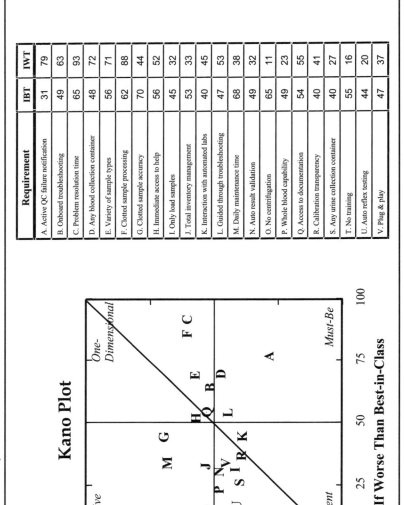

Requirement	IBT	IWT
A. Active QC failure notification	31	79
B. Onboard troubleshooting	49	63
C. Problem resolution time	65	93
D. Any blood collection container	48	72
E. Variety of sample types	56	71
F. Clotted sample processing	62	88
G. Clotted sample accuracy	70	44
H. Immediate access to help	56	52
I. Only load samples	45	32
J. Total inventory management	53	33
K. Interaction with automated labs	40	45
L. Guided through troubleshooting	47	53
M. Daily maintenance time	68	38
N. Auto result validation	49	32
O. No centrifugation	65	11
P. Whole blood capability	49	23
Q. Access to documentation	54	55
R. Calibration transparency	40	41
S. Any urine collection container	40	27
T. No training	55	16
U. Auto reflex testing	44	20
V. Plug & play	47	37

this example shows some very clear statements from the customer. The customer considers requirement A, active QC failure notification, a must-be requirement; the product should definitely satisfy this capability. Requirement L (the operator wants to be guided through troubleshooting) barely falls into the must-be category. The medical diagnostic company needs to analyze this requirement further, since its IBT score of 47 and IWT score of 53 indicates that there was a mixed response to this question.

ALL RESULTS ARE NOT CREATED EQUAL

The Kano mapping and analysis prepares the team to move on to the key activity in this stage of the MDPD process: prioritizing individual requirements. The mapping clearly identifies which requirements are must-be (it is essential that you fulfill them, but it is not necessary to do any better than everyone else), which are one-dimensional (you should be better than your competitors), and which are attractive (they would delight the customer and can be marketing "wows," but they aren't necessary if budget or schedule prohibit).

In examining each response, the team needs to identify and explain results that deviate significantly from the majority of responses, implying that different market segments or categories of respondents have different values. The team needs to not be afraid to jettison results that skew the data because the specific requirement was not relevant to individual respondents. Eliminating the results for a respondent set that does not include the target user when these results diverge from the norm can give you a truer picture of the customer requirements for your target market. In the example of the hypothetical desk manufacturer, teachers, administrators, and students (the user group for desks) responded as part of a survey of the education market. Students ranked the requirement (that desks sustain minimum damage) as indifferent, while teachers and administrators ranked the same requirement as a must-be. Since students are not the primary beneficiaries of desks that sustain minimum damage, whereas administrators do receive the benefit of longer-lasting desks, excluding the student results gives you a more accurate idea of the requirements considered essential by the people who will benefit from damage-proof desks. The scores of the teachers aren't necessarily relevant, but since they didn't differ from those of the primary beneficiaries, leaving their scores in the mix is not unreasonable.

By constructing Kano plots for each requirement, showing responses from all market segments and functions, you can determine whether deviant responses indicate true market differentiation. Results clustered together indicate that there isn't a significant difference across different market segments and respondents for a particular requirement, as shown in Figure 9.5, whereas widely dispersed results indicate the potential for requirement priorities differing among different market segments or types of respondent.

The Kano plot in Figure 9.6 shows technologists' and chemists' responses deviating from the group. This requirement—being able to use a maximum number of blood collection containers for a diagnostic chemical analyzer—is valued differently by the laboratory supervisors and managers, chemists, and technologists.

The technologists would be delighted if one system could handle a number of blood collection containers, but they could live without this feature because it doesn't affect the way they do their jobs. Other people in the hospital, such as the chemist who said that the system should be able to handle more containers, are affected more significantly. Chemists can recommend only a limited number of container types; if the system does not accept the type they recommend, they must change their recommendation. Supervisors and managers want a system that is at least on a par with the current equipment, since any reduction in the number of container sizes accepted might cost them more in increased preparation time and the need for additional containers for sample transfers.

In this case, the requirement was not relevant to technologists because it did not address something that the technologists considered a problem. The company doing this survey decided to remove the technologists' responses, since the technologists were not the primary users: They simply carry out the work and don't really care how many containers there are. In addition, to be conservative, the company considered this requirement to be one-dimensional. Using these data, the company

Figure 9.5. This Kano analysis for one customer requirement indicates that no significant differences exist across different segments.

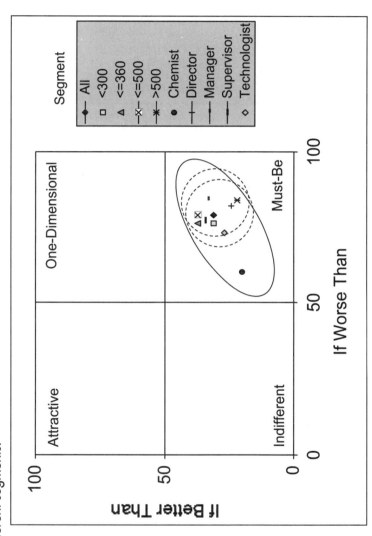

Figure 9.6. Kano analysis for one customer requirement with respondent differentiation.

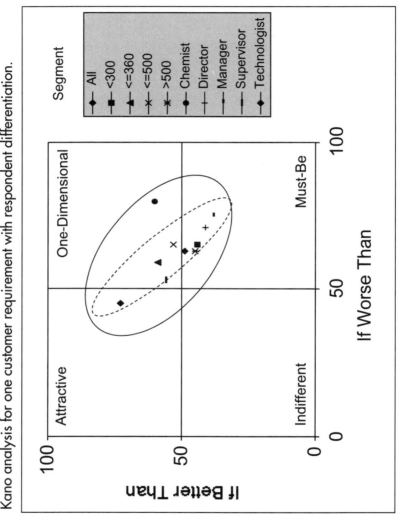

can intelligently decide how much risk it wants to take in supplying features that address this requirement.

Where there are different results for valid user sets, you need to determine if these differences might drive product options or modularization. Automobile companies have to deal with this type of decision on a regular basis. For example, suppose an automobile company surveyed customers in various geographic regions regarding car washing. Specifically, they examined the requirement that the car requires minimal washing. Survey results for different geographic segments would vary widely. In the Northeast, satisfying this requirement would be a delighter. In the South, respondents might be indifferent. In California, where water is scarce, this could be a must-be requirement. In the Midwest, the requirement could be one-dimensional: The less often you needed to wash this car compared to competing models, the more satisfied customers would be. Since satisfying this need could be very costly, an automobile manufacturer might lose significant market share in the South if it made the feature that provided this functionality part of its standard package. By making the feature optional, the company could serve each market optimally without losing market share.

ANALYZING EXISTING SOLUTIONS

Identifying and prioritizing customer requirements tells you how best to address those requirements. Adding context by defining and assessing alternative ways in which customers could satisfy each requirement will allow your team to understand exactly how to create products that are more desirable than competing products or existing solutions.

Traditional market research suggests simply evaluating competitors' products. That approach is too narrow. Your consideration of alternatives should include:

- All products you currently offer that meet one or more customer requirements.

- All competitive offerings that meet at least one customer requirement.

- All alternative approaches that customers currently use to meet the requirement. (For example, if you were developing the next generation mobile phone, your competition might include pagers, portable phones, personal digital assistants, and two-way radios.)

In Chapter 6, we emphasized the importance of developing requirements related to customer needs before and after purchase, in addition to the initial product experience. The same concept applies as you evaluate alternatives available to solve customer problems: existing solutions should be drawn from the entire consumption cycle, not just initial consumption.

Again, let's look at an automobile example. Figure 9.7 shows the consumption stages for a Saturn automobile. For Saturn, the buying experience and the owning experience are two of the most compelling points of the offer. Suppose Saturn was investigating the customer requirement to minimize the time it takes to service a car. If Saturn looked only at other car manufacturers as competitors, it might not consider the local garage, which may be able to service a local customer quite effectively. By extending its analysis of competitive service options, Saturn has created solutions—such as anniversary cards and annual get-

Figure 9.7. Solutions spanning the total consumption life cycle.

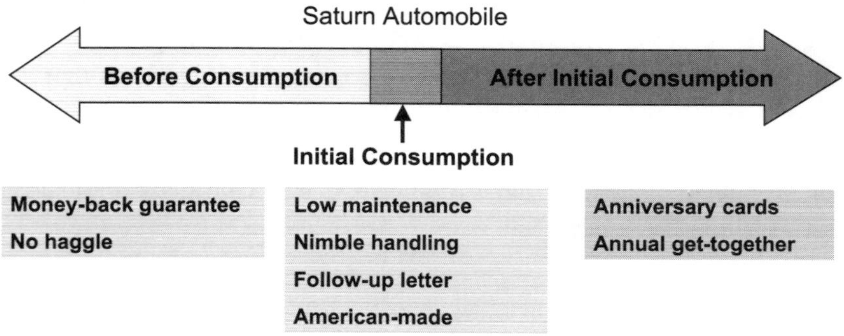

togethers—that encourage the car owner to choose the Saturn dealer over the local garage for service needs.

WEIGHTING SOLUTIONS RELATIVE TO THE BEST-IN-CLASS

Since not all existing solutions meet the customer's need to the same degree, we can use the weighting system described earlier in this chapter to assess each existing solution's ability to meet the requirement relative to the best-in-class solution. We assign a greater or lesser value to each existing solution based on the customer's degree of satisfaction, as shown in the sidebar.

If you understand the effectiveness of each existing solution in meeting the customer's requirements, you can determine how much work you need to do to provide the appropriate value to the customer. Some companies treat this process as a goal in itself, since it can provide some immediate benefits. By evaluating existing products against customer requirements, a company can determine the most effective positioning and sales strategies. (Salespeople love this type of information.) In addition, your product may provide features that your customers don't value. Knowing this, you might downplay these features in your current marketing activities and direct the dollars somewhere else. You don't have to wait until you launch the new product to benefit from understanding your customer's values.

Evaluating Existing Solutions Using a Weighted Matrix

The weighting system with the if-better-than and if-worse-than scores discussed earlier in the chapter highlights the relative value of each solution. Solutions that are worse than best-in-class receive a -1, whereas solutions that are the same as the existing best-in-class receive a 0. (Note that we don't use +1 here, because if a solution were better than the existing best-in-class, it would *be* the best-in-class. We employ the +1 rating in Chapter 10 when we brainstorm ways to better meet the customer requirements.) A solution that is scored with a 0 receives a weighted score of 0. We penalize solutions that are worse than the best-in-class by multiplying them by the if-worse-than weighting factor. The "raw" score column in the solution matrix (see Figure 9.8) depicts the −1, 0, +1 score. The weighted score is shown in the "Wgt" column.

The solution matrix (see Figure 9.8) allows you to understand very clearly the requirements that your product addresses *and* to compare your product to what your competitors are doing. Denise Flinn, Internet testing product manager of Teradyne's Broadband Test Division, explains it this way: "You can evaluate their competitive solutions against those requirements. . . . Because we're solving slightly different problems from those our competitors are solving, that helps us in our positioning of the product and saying, if this is the problem you want to solve, you should use our solution. It's really helped in establishing credibility because most often customers don't really spend that much time in understanding and analyzing their environment that we're trying to integrate solutions into."

DIVINING WHERE YOUR COMPETITORS ARE GOING

Your competition is not standing still while you are busy developing new products. How do you determine where your competition is today and where they are likely to be by the time you launch your new products?

Determining where your competitors will be going in the future is a lot harder. Analyzing your competitors' relative and absolute spending on research and development can help you do this. Has this amount changed over time, and is this change part of a trend? For public companies, you can find this information in annual reports. By examining several consecutive annual reports, you can determine the trend in R&D

Figure 9.8. The solution matrix enables the team to evaluate each existing solution.

REQUIREMENTS	#	Survey Results RSOR	IBT	IWT	Best in Class (BIC)	Existing Solution A R a w	Wgt	Existing Solution B R a w	Wgt	Existing Solution C R a w	Wgt	What To Do?	New Solution A R a w	Wgt	New Solution B R a w	Wgt	New Solution C R a w	Wgt
Requirement	18	0	50	25	C	-1	-25	-1	-25	0	0	Nothing						
Requirement	19	52	63	75	C	-1	-75	-1	-75	0	0	Better than BIC						
Requirement (Red level label)	20	0	63	50	None	-1	-50	-1	-50	-1	-50	As well as BIC						
Requirement	21	0	50	50	A	0	0	-1	-50	-1	-50	As well as BIC						
Requirement	22	0	50	100	C	-1	-100	-1	-100	0	0	As well as BIC						
Requirement (Red level label)	23	81	100	38	B	-1	-38	0	0	-1	-38	Nothing						
Requirement	24	112	100	63	C	-1	-63	-1	-63	0	0	Wow						
Requirement (Blue level label)	25	81	100	100	None	-1	-100	-1	-100	-1	-100	Better than BIC						
Requirement	26	0	13	0	None	-1	0	-1	0	-1	0	Nothing						
Total							-1088		-1075		-575							

141

spending. If your main competitors are not public companies, you can create your own chronological map showing when a company introduced new products and whether the products were variants of existing products, product line extensions, or truly new. Finally, research firms in your industry also may collect these data.

Your industry may not be as predictable as the semiconductor industry, which is guided by Moore's law,[1] but you can assess the direction in which you think your competitors will go by understanding their technology drivers. Technology drivers or core technologies are those that give a company an edge over competitive or alternative solutions. These key technologies can be used in technology trending graphs, competitive price versus performance analysis, and customer requirement work. For example, if you wanted to look at technology drivers in the diagnostic equipment industry, you could use competitors' data sheets to glean information from which you could chart the number of samples that could be processed per hour against the quality of the sample. Such a chart would tell you whether a competitor is driving its business on that dimension—whether it is a follower or a leader.

A price/performance trend map like the example in Figure 9.9 helps you evaluate the future positioning of both your products and your competitors' products. You can use trend mapping to estimate the rate of technological development in a particular industry. Looking ahead on the map helps you determine what features you will have to include at launch and provides a road map for future product developments. For example, in the trend map in Figure 9.9 your own product 3 is projected to beat your competitor's expected product C based on the application of the technology trend line.

Figure 9.10 is an example of trend mapping applied to operations. Such a map can help you deduce how your competition will be investing relative to improving operational performance. If they traditionally haven't kept up with you or others in a particular area, this area may not be their core competency.

Determining the slope of the technology curve in your industry is critical to knowing where the market is heading and how fast and who is likely to achieve the next breakthrough. The question is not *if* the technology in your industry will change, but *when* and by *how* much.

Figure 9.9. Competitive analysis trend map.

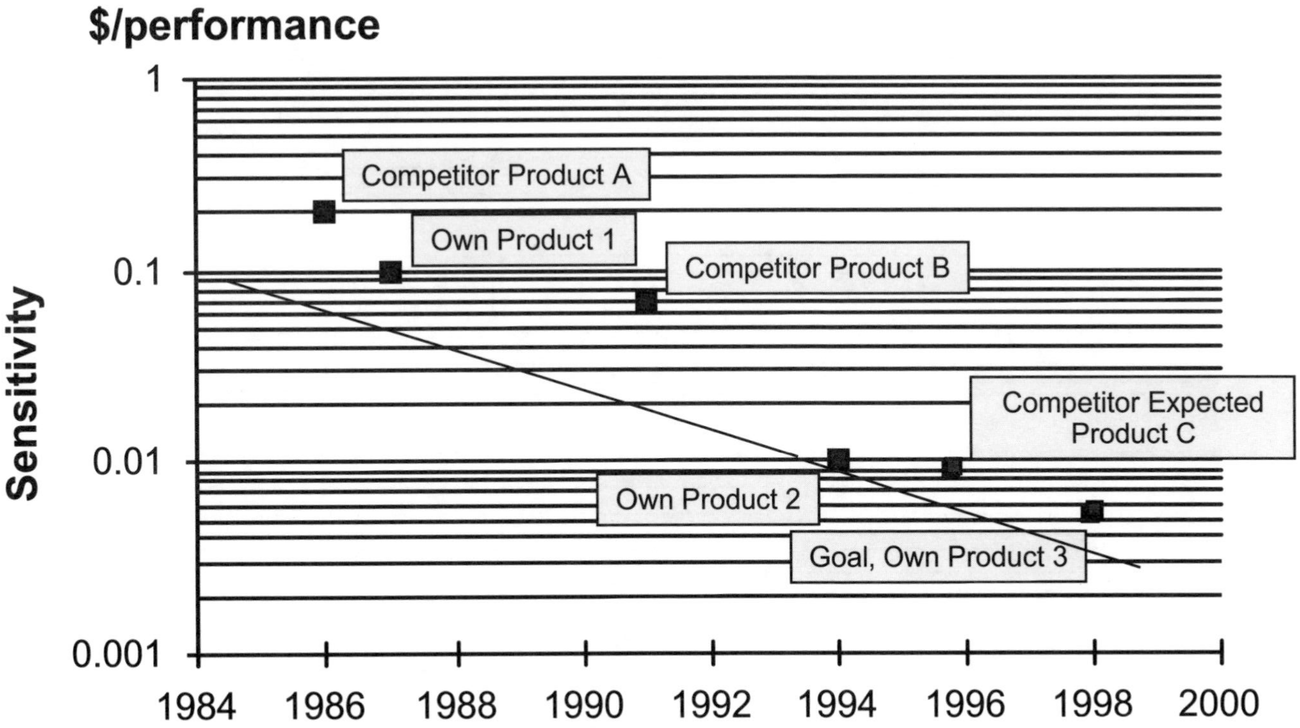

Figure 9.10. An operational trend map comparing a company's existing products with those of its competitors over time.

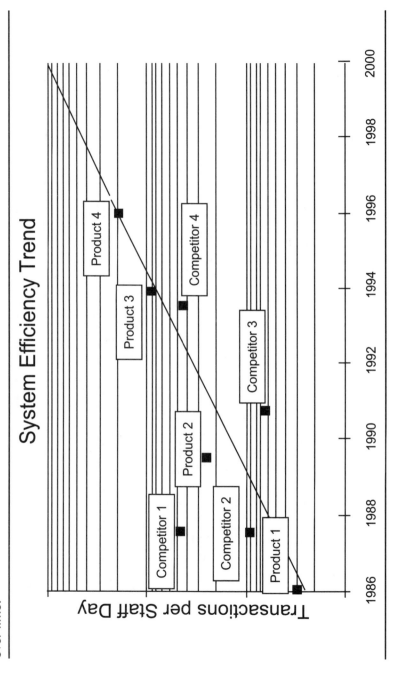

System Efficiency Trend

Transactions per Staff Day

Product 4

Product 3

Competitor 4

Competitor 3

Product 2

Competitor 1

Competitor 2

Product 1

1986   1988   1990   1992   1994   1996   1998   2000

Although predicting the trend in your industry requires a little crystal-ball gazing (in the form of mapping the rate of change in the technology trend), you will be in a much better position to anticipate change if you do this, rather than being unpleasantly surprised.

Mike Grant, business development manager for The Chinet Company, credits the MDPD process (known at Chinet as VOTC, or Voice of the Customer), with improving his company's understanding of competitive products. "Our knowledge of our competition increased considerably," he says. "Prior to the VOTC process we had done competitive testing and were aware of competitive products, but we didn't have a real specific regimen for testing and comparing our performance. . . . Through the VOTC process we did this for the product lines that were involved in our projects, but also it opened our eyes to the fact that we needed to take a more systematic approach to competitive analysis. We've gone on and done that as a result."

GETTING TO THE FINISH LINE

The concepts presented in this chapter helped you rank and analyze requirements. You now know which requirements your product needs to address, and to what degree it needs to address each one. If you are already the best-in-class in meeting a specific requirement, and if your trend and competitive analysis shows that your competitors are unlikely to move to match this requirement, you have an opportunity to focus your R&D dollars in another area. That is, include all the must-be requirements, but don't spend more than is necessary to satisfy them. Aim to match or slightly beat your competition on one-dimensional requirements, but avoid excess spending on them. You simply want to prevent a prospective customer from choosing a competitive product because you failed to satisfy the customers' needs in this area to the degree indicated in your survey. Don't take the chance that a competitor will provide greater satisfaction. Include some attractive requirements, which can differentiate your offering from your competition, help in product positioning, or be used to target unique market segments.

Now you are in a position to reap tangible rewards from the product definition process. By eliminating requirements that are perceived as indifferent and not spending too much on must-bes, you can lower overall product development costs.

Knowing what customers value and how you and your competition measures up against the requirements tells you how to make a product that will delight the customer. The final step in the product definition process, and the subject of Chapter 10, is to brainstorm ideas and develop the most innovative, creative, and total solution to your customers' requirements.

1O

FROM OPPORTUNITY TO SOLUTION

Generating Creative Ideas

"Progress lies not in enhancing what is, but in advancing toward what will be."

—Kahlil Gibran

TURNING OPPORTUNITIES INTO POTENTIAL SOLUTIONS

The intensive activities in the first three stages of the MDPD process—preparing for customer visits, processing visit data, and analyzing customer requirements—have revealed exactly what customers need. Now the team must figure out the best combination of product attributes to satisfy those needs: In other words, it must turn the requirements into solutions.

The goal of the fourth and final stage of the MDPD process is to create a manageable set of solutions in a form that is easy to evaluate. Brainstorming—an idea-generation technique that has been used by almost everyone in business at some point—is by no means the only way to generate solutions. This chapter presents a variety of methods for generating the broadest range of creative solutions. Chapter 11 discusses how to evaluate the solutions and choose the best one.

BEEN THERE, DONE THAT

The biggest risk in including a chapter on developing innovative solutions is that most people in business believe that they already do this through technology innovation. The attitude that "only engineers have ideas worth considering, so why do something with a cross-functional team?" tends to coincide with the attitude that "we know our customers' requirements." Both outlooks severely limit a company's ability to create valuable products that delight customers.

If you are confident that your organization is best-in-class in terms of innovation, ask whether the innovations meet customer requirements. Most companies brainstorm solutions from the perspective of the technical discipline of the brainstormer. The mechanical engineers come up with ideas for the housing of the product, the electrical engineers innovate around the electronics, marketers think about services, technical writers think about manuals, and the software engineers come up with creative ways to build the software. What is missing is the holistic view—the cross-functional product development focus on meeting customer requirements.

The purpose of brainstorming as described in this chapter is to generate ideas and develop the building blocks for the most innovative and creative solutions to customer requirements by testing the boundaries of what seems possible.

In its most basic form, brainstorming requires only a chalkboard or flipchart pad, some writing instruments, and a group of willing participants. Brainstorming groups are most effective if they are limited to about a dozen people. Limiting time periods to two-hour sessions helps keep the participants—and the ideas—fresh, although there may be times when a group will spend a whole day or even a week brainstorming.

Brainstorming sessions are effective only if there are clear goals. This is why it is so important to prioritize the hundreds of customer voices collected from the interview process to the vital twenty or thirty and to establish metrics to eliminate ambiguity. However, while the efforts of the brainstorming group should be narrowly focused, the purpose of the session is to generate as many ideas as possible—quantity, not quality, is the key.

Maintaining the involvement of the participants is a key prerequisite for success. Participants' minds tend to wander while one person presents an idea. Facilitators of idea brainstorming sessions frequently give participants things to occupy their hands and add a note of playfulness to the environment. For example, Silly Putty and Koosh balls enable participants to play mindlessly, keeping their hands busy and their minds creatively focused but not consumed. Silly Putty can be molded, pulled, rolled, and stretched for hours; Koosh balls have loops made of rubber band–like material and can be pulled, bounced, and tossed. Although these activities may appear frivolous, they can add to the team spirit and get the creative juices flowing.

Remember, too, that not all team members may be enthusiastic about the brainstorming process. The team leader may need to exercise his or her powers of persuasion to ensure participation. Ken Reindel, formerly at Keithley Instruments, recalls his experience with the engineering staff during the brainstorming portion of the MDPD process. "A number of the engineers in the room were saying 'This is baloney. What am I here for? I should be doing design.' That was difficult. I spent significant time offline with those people, talking to them and asking for their participation and cooperation with it."

BEYOND GENERIC BRAINSTORMING TO SOLUTION BRAINSTORMING

The principles of generic brainstorming apply to brainstorming product solutions, but fostering the highest degree of creativity and innovation requires some extra attention. Varying the brainstorming approach helps to maintain a high level of innovation. For example, participants might draw pictures, create analogies, construct metaphors, or tell stories. The session might involve each participant getting up to draw his or her idea on a whiteboard, or participants might all write down their ideas simultaneously, then share them.

Solution brainstorming is best done at the individual requirement level. This allows the participants to ignore any constraints that other requirements might impose on the solution. For example, suppose you are developing a new cellular phone. One requirement is the ability to use the phone for a maximum amount of time without connecting it to a power source, and another requirement is that the user can fit the phone in a maximum number of locations. Solutions related to power might require a larger phone that would be more difficult to fit in many locations. If participants are free to explore the power source solutions without regard to size constraints, you benefit from greater, unfettered creativity.

One way to encourage creativity is to have the group accept *every* idea, no matter how silly or impossible it may seem. Avoid criticism and judgment; delay the process of judging, refining, and testing the best ideas until *after* the brainstorming session.

A particularly useful method of recording ideas is to have participants draw a picture of the idea (solution) on a flip chart. People tend to resist this at first, but once someone gets the process going, the ideas flow rapidly and can be added to easily. After each participant finishes a picture, the group says in unison, "That's a good idea." This may sound corny, but it works—it encourages the free flow of ideas and induces participants to generate ideas fearlessly. *Any* criticism will stifle creativity and inhibit participants from generating ideas.

When participants sketch ideas, they also state the strengths of those ideas. You need a way to encourage participants to build and improve on an idea's strengths. There is a natural tendency to point out weaknesses in an idea by fixing what seems to be wrong, which may work in everyday life but which stifles the creative spirit necessary for productive brainstorming. Instead, participants should try to expand on or modify seemingly wild ideas rather than generating new ones. Only when one idea has been completely fleshed out should the team start work on another idea.

One approach to stimulating out-of-the-box thinking (described more fully in the sidebar below) is to ask the participants to think of ideas that might get them fired, are considered technically impossible, or would make them a laughingstock in the marketplace. For example, propose manufacturing metal doors in a company that specializes in manufacturing only wood doors. It is amazing to see how the team might expand a solution that initially seemed not to be technically feasible to arrive at an "Aha! We can do that!" moment.

Thinking Outside the Box

In the last few years, the phrase *thinking outside of the box* has become a cliché. That has not diminished its importance for the creative process. Thinking outside the box means allowing your thoughts to range freely, without the constraints imposed by the traditional, conventional, known, or ritualistic solutions. It means exploring what-if scenarios: What if the idea is expanded, shrunk, frozen, dehydrated, melted, or heated? What if you can do what no one else does—fly or type 1,000 words per minute? What is the worst or best possible outcome?

Creativity is rooted in viewing a problem in different ways and from varying perspectives. A simple puzzle—aptly in the form of a box—demonstrates the point. In the diagram that follows, the challenge is to connect all the dots without lifting your pen or pencil from the paper or retracing your path.

When most people attempt to visualize connecting the dots, the box framed by the dots seems to constrain them, making it impossible for them to see a solution. Such logical left-brain, straight-ahead, inside-the-box thinking is ineffective in generating ideas for how to solve the problem. Only by stepping *outside* the box can we begin to envision the solution:

The solution shown is a form of lateral thinking.[1] It seeks to solve a problem by exploring multiple possibilities—by changing perceptions or concepts or by generating new ones.

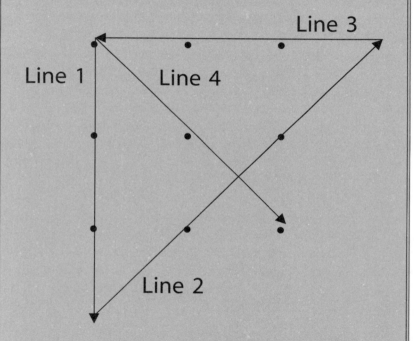

Attacking a problem with brute force is not conducive to lateral thinking or tangential thought. If you find yourself frustrated with a line of thinking, come at the problem from different directions or perspectives. Rotate it; turn it backward, sideways, or upside down. In brainstorming sessions, we encourage outside guests from a relevant area to participate in order to provide a different

> perspective. Outside experts in a brainstorming session will bring different areas of knowledge to bear on the problem. If you don't think laterally, you can be assured that a competitor will.

WHOM TO INVOLVE?

The core participants in solution brainstorming are members of the development team. As suggested in the sidebar above, inviting experts from both within and outside the company can greatly enhance the process. Progressive customers, lead users, vendors, key suppliers, consultants, or technical staff members outside the team add many new dimensions that will drive creativity.

Lead users may not be in your discipline, but they have expertise in solving similar customer requirements in other industries. For example, if you were developing a room purifier, you might invite people who have designed clean-room environments for semiconductor processing, where ventilation specifications are considerably more stringent. The clean-room designers have already solved the problem for a certain set of specifications, and they can contribute ideas at a different level of maturity. Similarly, when the development team from 3M was creating special sandpaper for curved edges, they invited sculptors and construction companies that specialized in restoration of old homes to participate in solution brainstorming. These individuals had experience in solving this problem and could provide fresh, new insights into the issues involved.

Participants who have not been involved in the MDPD process and are not familiar with the customer requirements will benefit from reviewing the image and requirement diagrams, the competitive analysis, and the prioritization of requirements. This information provides an important backdrop to the brainstorming session. In fact, how you decide to handle each requirement can affect the level of brainstorming. After you prioritize customer requirements and evaluate existing solutions (both competitive and nontraditional), you decide whether you need to do anything more with your current product (if you have one), whether you need to do a little better than the best-in-class solution, whether you need to do a lot better, or whether you could ignore this requirement altogether. If the requirement is a must-be, but your solution already is best-in-class, you don't need to enhance it. Likewise, if the customer is indifferent to the requirement, you can focus the brainstorming activities on other requirements that demand greater innovation—the ones that will differentiate your product.

ALTERNATIVES TO BRAINSTORMING

There is no blueprint for creative thinking and idea generation; there are only methods for stimulating the process, of which brainstorming is one. Discontinuity in routine is another method: Deliberately interrupt or distract yourself; take a walk; take your mother's advice and *sleep on it*. Creating a pause allows the problem to remain just below the level of consciousness and frequently leads to solutions while the thinker is doing something else.

Exploring alternatives helps to generate ideas: If the freeway is hopelessly clogged with traffic, take surface streets; alter your destination; reschedule, delay, or cancel your appointment; take a helicopter; or initiate a videoconference.

The Forced Analogies Technique

The mind can visualize similarities between most situations, people, objects, or events. The forced analogies technique makes use of this capacity and can foster creativity by comparing a problem with a dissimilar thing. For example, suppose a customer requirement is "to maximize the time the laptop computer is operational" (to limit the number of times it crashes, minimize repair time, and return it to operation as quickly as possible). How is this requirement like those for the Pathfinder spacecraft sent on a mission to Mars? The Pathfinder spacecraft must have all its subsystems monitored—fuel, solar panels, inside and outside temperature, attitude, trajectory, telemetry equipment—and must radio numerous telemetric data to Earth. The spacecraft needs to be self-diagnostic. It must be capable of withstanding the rigors of introduction into space, travel through space, and landing on Mars. All systems must operate flawlessly, but they also must incorporate redundancy of mission-critical subsystems, since a single error can preempt thousands of functions that were performed faultlessly, and only one mistake can be catastrophic to the mission.

Having the development team explore the requirements for the Pathfinder spacecraft may give rise to ideas that might apply to laptop computers. They may explore ideas for incorporating more self-diagnostics or including remote wireless diagnostics direct from the manufacturer's technical support centers. Automatic backup and redundant subsystems such as software or flash memory hard drives with internal firewalls may make disk crashes and computer viruses obsolete. Solar power panels may augment battery operation.

Storyboarding

Another useful technique for generating possible solutions to customer requirements is *storyboarding*. Storyboarding can facilitate team communication, stimulate ideas, and coordinate the team's work. The technique is used frequently in advertising to manage scenes in television commercials and focus discussions. The process helps participants fit the pieces together, see unique connections, and understand what needs to be accomplished next. The process starts with a basic topic, then subtopics expanding on the basic topic are created. The subtopics are then further expanded to refine and illustrate the idea.

Learning From the Past: The TRIZ Technique

Brainstorming is a freewheeling creative process for generating random ideas. The antithesis of this technique is TRIZ. (TRIZ is the Russian acronym for the Theory of Inventive Problem Solving.) Genrich Saulovich Altshuller, who worked in the patent office of what was then the Soviet Union, developed TRIZ beginning in 1946. Altshuller and his colleagues screened 1,500,000 worldwide patents looking for inventive solutions to problems. Altshuller began categorizing these patents in a way that removed the industry classification (such as automotive or printing) to reveal the underlying problem-solving process. He found that true innovations often used science from outside the field in which they were developed. He also discovered that the same problems had been repeatedly solved in different industries. Altshuller discovered that more than 90 percent of the problems engineers faced had previously been solved in some industry somewhere else.[2] This laid the foundation for the development of an analytical method governed by certain laws or principles to solve inventive problems, later known as TRIZ.

Some TRIZ practitioners who emigrated from the Soviet Union introduced TRIZ in the United States in the mid-1980s. The technique captured the attention of the business world during the 1990s. Initially, companies used TRIZ to improve a single product or process; later, they extended its use to strategic company issues and industry trends.[3] Ford Motor Company, General Motors, Exxon Mobil, Procter & Gamble, Hewlett-Packard, and other *Fortune* 500 companies have used the TRIZ methodology.

TRIZ begins with the hypothesis that there is a set of principles that underlies all creative innovations and that identifying these principles makes the process of invention more predictable. These forty or so inventive principles are then used to develop an invention along an evolutionary path.

Companies can apply TRIZ to solve important customer requirements, particularly when the team has hit a roadblock. However, if the solution involves applying breakthrough concepts, companies need to evaluate the learning curve and investment risk. As shown in Figure 10.1, the level of technical and financial risk increases in proportion to the effort and knowledge required for a given solution. Incremental product enhancements carry low risk; at the other end of the spectrum are solutions requiring knowledge outside of the company's R&D department, solutions requiring knowledge outside of its industry, and areas requiring breakthrough research.

Figure 10.1. Relative risk levels for different types of solutions.

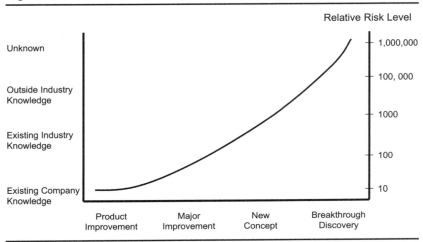

Examine a Database of Solutions

Companies can use a database of prior solutions for analogous problems (derived from case studies) to expand the pool of potential solutions. (For example, the TRIZ method was developed using case studies of patents available in the federal archives of the former Soviet Union.) For this information to be valuable, the team must examine each case study closely to determine the dimensions of the problem. Software packages that document problems enable users to input the parameters of a problem and retrieve information about how analogous problems have been solved.

Don't Do It Just Once

Finally, teams should treat the idea-generation process as iterative. Once you have evaluated the concepts as described in Chapter 11, it may make sense to revisit some of the solutions, either to increase their customer value or to identify different partners and/or new ways of providing the solutions.

THE VALUE OF VALUE

Although this chapter has used the word *solution*, the focus has been on addressing an individual requirement. Once the team has generated ideas for each of the requirements, it can combine the ideas into customer solutions. To do this effectively, the team must understand not only what customers say they want, but what they *value*—what they will pay to own or use.

A solution that addresses the right customer requirements in the right way is inherently complete, customer-focused, and big-picture. A good test of whether a solution incorporates all the necessary require- ments is to ask whether the solution contains elements that the company currently cannot deliver. If the company can deliver everything, then the focus is probably too narrow and the solution will not deliver value to the customer. The Harley-Davidson story that follows describes the importance of focusing solution brainstorming sessions on customers' requirements and understanding what constitutes value for the cus- tomer.

Harley-Davidson, Inc., knows that the only way to truly understand the customer experience is to have it yourself. Harley employees have gotten very close to customers by actually experiencing the customers' lifestyle, including riding with them rain or shine. Harley-Davidson es- tablished the Harley Owner Group, now the largest motorcycle club in the world,[4] as a way of communicating with its customers. The company launched new product development programs with the emphasis on delivering value to the customer. As a result, after facing near-extinction in the early 1980s, Harley engineered a total turnaround. In 2000, the firm enjoyed its fifteenth consecutive year of record growth.[5]

Harley turned around and redefined its business by understanding what its end customers value—not just the tangible aspects of the prod- uct, but the lifestyle and culture that surrounds what is known as the Harley experience. Harley has such brand loyalty that customers will tattoo the company logo on their bodies—a testament to how far the company goes to deliver customer value. Customers *want* transporta- tion, but they *value* a lifestyle expression. Consequently, Harley doesn't just create a quality motorcycle; it helps customers create a piece of art. Honda Motor Company and Yamaha Motor Corporation produce high-quality Harley knockoffs, but they have not captured the hearts and minds of their owners. Because everyone at Harley, from the CEO down, understands the customer at a deep level, the company can envision and develop products that consistently bring value to customers and profit to Harley.

This chapter has discussed a number of ways to develop potential solutions: involving lead users, academics, and others outside your team to bring in fresh perspectives; eliminating the normal limitations on what you do or don't do by engaging in creative brainstorming techniques; and, most significantly, thinking about how to create value. In Chapter 11, we discuss the final step in the MDPD process: identifying the single best solution and honing it to meet customer needs in the form of a product or service that provides true value to customers.

11

HITTING THE MARKET'S SWEET SPOT

Selecting Solutions That Customers Value

"Results are gained not by solving problems, but by exploiting opportunities."

—Peter Drucker

MAKING THE HARD CHOICES

The product definition process is nearly complete. The team knows which requirements will satisfy customers and to what degree, has evaluated existing and competitive solutions against metrics developed for each of these requirements, and understands which existing products are worse than or the same as the best-in-class product. Brainstorming and other creative techniques have generated a variety of potential solutions. Now the team's focus becomes selecting the optimal solution or solutions to meet the customers' requirements.

The method used to evaluate solutions for customer requirements can be creatively random or dogmatically systematic, depending on the circumstances surrounding the problem, the scope of the project, the importance of the project to the company, and the business case. Using survey results, involving customers, and techniques such as conjoint analysis can all contribute to the evaluation process. These methods alone, however, are not enough. Any decision about which requirements the solution will address, and to what extent it will address these requirements, *must* include an assessment of customer value. Those requirements that provide little value to the customer need close scrutiny, since spending product development funds on them is not likely to generate adequate returns. Concentrating R&D expenditures on the solutions that satisfy your customers' missing functionality *in areas that those customers value* allows product differentiators, and the marketing positioning that follows as a natural consequence, to emerge.

The goal, of course, is to decide how to allocate the development budget in order to produce the greatest return for the company. Steve Binder, director of technology development at Bio-Rad Laboratories' Clinical Diagnostics Group, summarized his MDPD experience this way: "If the customers were indifferent, we certainly were not going to spend a lot of money on those requirements. And if it's a must-be requirement, you spend only enough to meet the minimum requirement in the field and save your engineering dollars for the bells and whistles. The whole point of the process is to tell you how to spend your money, to tell you the features that are likely to get you sales, and to tell you the features that customers don't care about, so you don't overspend in those areas."

"MDPD was used to define the critical features of the instruments we manufacture," Binder says. "For example, we found out that certain features that we felt were really important to customers (although they were relevant to them) were much less important than we originally thought. While some features were relevant, very few customers would make buying decisions based on them. One person on the team was totally focused on appearance. He thought it was extremely important. But as it turned out, the process uncovered the fact that all customers agreed that appearance was *not* important. It wasn't even close. We learned that customers would never buy based on appearance. They care if it does the job or not—not how it looks. Without the process, we might have gone down the wrong path if we had listened to the well-intentioned vocal member of the team whose perceptions were not in line with customer requirements. On the other hand, we confirmed that the customers' highest concerns related to serviceability and reliability. That translated to very clear instructions to engineering on how to allocate resources."

INVOLVING CUSTOMERS

Customer involvement in the evaluation of alternative concepts can be quite valuable. This can be done through customer advisory boards, by going back to customers who were visited earlier, or by using a professional organization to run focus groups. Depending on the level of research and development required to implement the proposed solution, creating a prototype may be necessary.

The virtual world is playing an increasingly significant role in obtaining customer feedback, as Chapter 12 details. Companies now conduct focus groups online. Some use sophisticated CAD software to build prototypes that customers can evaluate. Several organizations are moving toward virtual reality capabilities to enhance customers' experience of potential products. Massachusetts Institute of Technology (MIT) worked with General Motors to get customer feedback by simulating the experience of driving an electric car. This type of simulation is beginning to be available on the Web and eventually will become the standard approach.

CONJOINT ANALYSIS

Some companies use a technique known as *conjoint analysis* at this stage. Conjoint analysis is a marketing research technique that can provide valuable information for making feature selection decisions, especially if the product will be offered in various combinations and you need to know which combinations will best meet the needs of various market segments. Potential buyers examine and evaluate a range of features or attributes and choose which combinations they like best. Conjoint analy-

sis examines the trade-offs to determine what feature combinations purchasers value most. A company can conduct a number of choice
simulations to estimate market share for products with different attributes or features.

Carole Katz, director of market research and analysis at Avaya, Inc.
(formerly Lucent Technologies), describes her experience with this evaluation process: "We said, let's prioritize the requirements: what are the
attractives, what are the must haves. Then we generate the concepts and
go out and validate with the customers. Did we get the requirements
right? Technology now enables us to get a picture up on the Web. You
click here, you open it up, and there's a picture of the concept, a description of the concept, a little boilerplate on what it is. Now we can do
something more akin to traditional conjoint analysis: Which of these
might you be interested in purchasing? We could do some trade-offs to
see if any of these concepts seem to meet the customer's needs."

Carole continues: "It's a very, very high-level first-order thumbs
up, thumbs down around the concept. But what it has allowed us to do
is bring the project to completion faster because usually there's lag time
in waiting for the research results to come back. And then the team has
early input on the concept that they can drive into their business case
work in the next phase."

Based on the results of this activity, you can re-rate the satisfaction
that each alternative solution for the requirement provides. Namely,
given the metric, how well does the solution meet the requirement? An
alternative solutions matrix like the one in Figure 11.1 can help the team
focus on the best solutions and provide insight into positioning the product in the competitive landscape.

VALUE MAPPING AS A TECHNIQUE FOR PRIORITIZING SOLUTIONS

The team must ultimately select the optimum set of solutions, using all
the information on the solutions matrix introduced later in this chapter.
One way to do this is to create a *value map* of the potential solutions. A

Figure 11.1. The completed solution matrix quickly identifies how the optimal solutions and the competitors are rated on specific customer requirements. Existing and new solutions have been rated, and weighting factors from a Kano survey have been used to develop a score.

	REQUIREMENTS	#	Survey Results RSOR	IBT	IWT	Best in Class (BIC)	Existing Solution A Raw	Wgt	Existing Solution B Raw	Wgt	Existing Solution C Raw	Wgt	What To Do?	New Solution A Raw	Wgt	New Solution B Raw	Wgt	New Solution C Raw	Wgt
	Requirement	18	0	50	25	C	-1	-25	-1	-25	0	0	Nothing	-1	-25	-1	-25	-1	-25
	Requirement	19	52	63	75	C	-1	-75	-1	-75	0	0	Better than BIC	1	63	1	63	0	0
Blue level label	Requirement	20	0	63	50	None	-1	-50	-1	-50	-1	-50	As well as BIC	0	0	1	63	0	0
Red level label	Requirement	21	0	50	50	A	0	0	-1	-50	-1	-50	As well as BIC	1	50	1	50	0	0
	Requirement	22	0	50	100	C	-1	-100	-1	-100	0	0	As well as BIC	0	0	-1	-100	0	0
Red level label	Requirement	23	81	38	38	B	-1	-38	0	0	-1	-38	Nothing	-1	-38	-1	-38	-1	-38
Blue level label	Requirement	24	112	100	63	C	-1	-63	-1	-63	0	0	Wow	1	100	1	100	0	0
	Requirement	25	81	100	100	None	-1	-100	-1	-100	-1	-100	Better than BIC	0	0	1	100	0	0
	Requirement	26	0	13	0	None	-1	0	-1	0	-1	0	Nothing	-1	0	-1	0	-1	0
	Total							-1088		-1075		-575			625		388		200

value map (see sidebar below and Figure 11.2) is an interactive tool that is used to review and revise solutions in order to ensure that the optimum portfolio of solutions has been created. Plotting potential product solutions on a value map helps companies prioritize product development programs by assessing variables that really matter.

Value Mapping

Value mapping is a technique for understanding the optimum solution to a set of customer requirements. To create a value map, you plot customer value versus both your investment (cost) and your return. Plotting in three dimensions enables you to account for both cost and the value of the product to the firm. A value map plots the following:

- *Customer value* is the combination of the degree to which a solution meets a customer's total needs (for a given set of markets) and the solution's degree of difference from the competition. These numbers are the totals for the best solutions for which customers have expressed specific requirements.

- *Cost* is the total cost to develop the solution; this can be estimated using range estimates or analogies to prior programs or developed in more detail prior to this analysis.

- *Return to the company* is defined as the profits and intangible company benefits that are accrued as a result of the solution. The intangible benefits must be converted to a value and added to the profit. For example, although Hewlett-Packard never made much money on calculators, it captured the mind share of a generation of engineers, who now buy only HP test equipment because of their experience with HP calculators. The return on HP's investment in calculators includes this intangible benefit.

- *The sweet spot* is the place on the value map where high customer value, high return to the company, and low cost converge. When you find the *sweet spot,* you will have identified the payoff for all the hard work that went into the MDPD process.

Only after plotting a solution on the value map do you evaluate organizational and architectural constraints. This way, available resources or technology never constrain solutions.

ASSESSING CONSTRAINTS

Finally, the team must consider all the constraints imposed by the solution. Does existing manufacturing capacity exist, or are new manufacturing facilities required? Does the company have the technological capability in place? What are the technical risks? Is adequate capital fund-

Figure 11.2. The value map plots a portfolio of solutions against their value to the customer and the internal return and cost. The relative size of the circle represents the financial value to the firm, with larger circles having higher value.

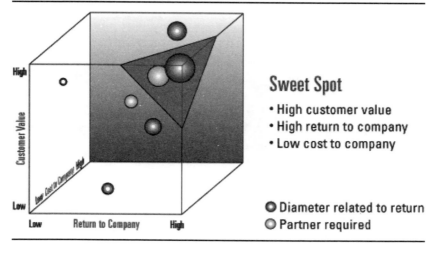

Sweet Spot
• High customer value
• High return to company
• Low cost to company

⦾ Diameter related to return
◯ Partner required

ing available? Are working prototypes required? What is the time schedule or time constraint? Does the necessary marketing capability exist? Are existing distribution channels adequate?

These constraints generally will be bounded by the scope of the project; the market opportunity being pursued; the investment required; the technical, marketing, and financial risks involved; the expected returns; competitive positioning; and the overall business case. Figure 11.3 shows a portion of a completed matrix.

ASSESSING SOLUTIONS IN THE CONTEXT OF THE PRODUCT LIFE CYCLE

To determine value, managers must really understand deeply what consumers will pay for and how much they will pay. Typically, however, most managers focus on the discrete or tangible product, as opposed to solutions that address customer needs from a much wider perspective. One way to view this wider perspective is to look at the consumption life cycle, an idea introduced in Chapter 6 and discussed further in Chapter 9. The consumption life cycle includes a period before the initial use of the product or service and may include specification, configuration, and customization.

Solutions should include delivery, installation, and break-in. At the point of initial consumption, the product is put into productive use. After this initial consumption period, maintenance, repair, upgrades, refurbishment, recertification, disposal, and recycling occur.

Most managers believe that a product delivers maximum value during the period of initial consumption, when the purchaser first experiences the product or service and puts it to use. However, there are many cases in which most of the value is not delivered at this point. For example, as explained in Chapter 9, for Saturn the buying experience is one of the most compelling points of the offer. For Mercedes, there are many *post*-consumption value drivers, including roadside assistance anywhere, anytime.

Figure 11.3. The requirements matrix incorporates constraints and risks associated with proposed solutions.

Require-ment	#	ALL			Segment 1			Segment 2			What To Do?	Solution 1		Solution 2		Solution 3		Solution 4	
		RSOR	IBT	IWT	RSOR	IBT	IWT	RSOR	IBT	IWT		RAW	WGT	RAW	WGT	RAW	WGT	RAW	WGT
Blue Label / Red Label	1	368	48	41	135	42	49	44	54	29	Nothing	0	0	-1	-49	0	0	0	0
	2	45	41	35	23	35	37	21	43	39	Nothing	-1	-37	-1	-37	1	35	1	35
	3	456	52	33	135	45	33	96	60	30	Nothing	-1	-33	-1	-33	1	45	1	45
	4	108	54	37	23	48	30	69	61	38	WOW	1	61	1	61	0	0	1	61
Blue Label / Red Label	5	1596	70	51	168	61	48	420	67	53	Parity +	1	67	0	0	1	66	0	0
	6	108	63	47	0	48	48	21	66	45	WOW	1	66	0	0	1	66	0	0
	7	108	50	36	0	33	40	0	53	42	WOW	1	53	-1	-42	-1	-42	0	0
	8	621	57	40	104	49	35	21	59	39	WOW	1	59	0	0	1	59	0	0
													540		-70		301		-209

	Solution 1	Solution 2	Solution 3	Solution 4
Technical risk	H	L	M	L
Product cost	$100	$90	$95	$95
Development cost	H	L	M	L
Resource skill	OK	OK	OK	OK
Schedule	9mths	6mths	6mths	6mths
Capital cost	$1M	$.5M	$.75M	$.5M
Manufacturing risk	L	M	L	L

ASSESSING SOLUTIONS THAT INCLUDE NONPRODUCT AUGMENTATIONS

Another important consideration in assessing solutions is to study the entire product, not just the tangible portion. Carole Katz of Avaya, Inc., discovered this when she was assessing customer requirements related to a strategic project involving convergence issues in the communications market. Approximately two-thirds of the requirements from Avaya's market (customers and noncustomers) focused on the augmented product, which involved partnerships and relationships, rather than on the core product.

One excellent example of an augmented product that provides the best solution is an offer from Gateway, Inc. Initially, the purchase of a Gateway computer included installation. As the inclusion of installation moved along the continuum from an attractive attribute toward a must-be feature, Gateway augmented its offering. Gateway now not only included installation but offered to transfer a customer's existing files to the new computer.

Keep in mind all the possible nonproduct augmentations to your offering, as shown in Figure 11.4.

Another good example of the total product concept comes from The Chinet Company, a global marketer of premium disposable service and tableware products to the retail and food-service markets. Fast-food outlets are a major market segment for many of Chinet's products. During an interview to identify requirements for this market segment, a quick-serve store manager related that she was always trying to find ways to boost sales. She had successfully generated incremental business by developing, on her own, promotional programs geared toward local schools, groups, and associations. Chinet recognized a need (for local promotional items) and an opportunity to augment its product line. With a couple of national restaurant chains, Chinet developed promotional materials and marketing programs using the creative talent in Chinet's existing marketing group. The program was very successful. Chinet enhanced its value to one of its market segments by offering more than just products for delivering fast food to customers.

Figure 11.4. In mature markets, looking at the total product enables better competitive differentiation.

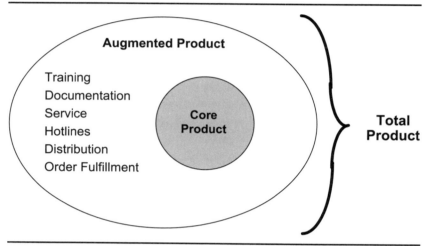

SOLUTIONS ALIGNED WITH STRATEGY

Rarely are enterprises equally adroit in all activities. Thus, they develop deeper competencies in a given area, upon which they then tend to focus their strategies. For example, Hewlett-Packard, Texas Instruments, Medtronics, Teradyne, and Apple, among many others, were developed and grew as companies with a focus on technological prowess, whereas others, such as Dell, Procter & Gamble, and 3M, were more focused on developing marketing expertise. Still others, such as General Electric, Maytag, and Caterpillar, concentrated on operational excellence.

Companies must consider the strategy of the enterprise when selecting among competing solutions. It should be obvious that the optimum solutions to satisfy customer requirements are those that align best with the strategy and culture of the organization. This is not to imply that competency in a particular area overrides the need to address the customer's explicit requirements; it simply states that organizational focus should be a factor to consider when evaluating potential solutions.

Every successful company has established a clear strategy and mission to focus the organization's efforts in a given direction. The solutions

Figure 11.5. The strategic focus of an organization influences solution choices. The large triangle shows each functional organization as equal, while the smaller triangles are more realistic variations.

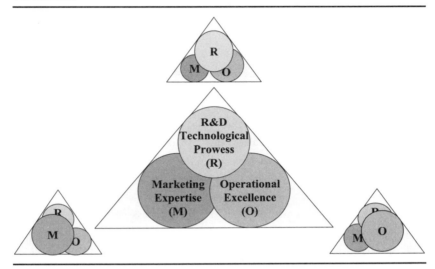

that have the greatest probability of successful implementation are those that are aligned with the company's strategy. Figure 11.5 graphically represents the extremes of organizational competencies and the real-world variations that can occur. Identifying the model that best represents your organization will allow you to align your solutions to the strategy, culture, and competencies of your organization for the greatest success. Establishing priorities among these areas, and following through on them when selecting solutions, will help to provide critical organizational alignment.

DEVELOPING FOR DIFFERENTIATION

When the MDPD process has identified attractive requirements that can be easily incorporated into the product, the job of selecting a solution that will wow the customer is easier. Depending on the type of product, you may be able to develop an initial product that incorporates solutions with limited complexity for a set of requirements identified as attractive. Subsequent releases of the product can then expand on the functionality to meet the attractive requirements more robustly. The later releases might be more complex, requiring more time and involving greater risk.

When no attractive requirements have been identified, it becomes more difficult to differentiate with product features alone. In mature markets, for example, differentiation is best achieved by looking at the total augmented product, not just at the core product, as described earlier in this chapter. Altering the required sequence of operation or the number of steps in the process can also be a differentiator. Recall the experience of Bio-Rad Laboratories, related by Steve Binder in Chapter 1, with the sequence of operation of its instrument. When the machine stopped with some test results complete and others incomplete, the machine, which was identical to most of the competitive instruments in operation, would not release the results of the completed tests until the problem was fixed. Through the MDPD process, Bio-Rad discovered that virtually all customers in the market felt strongly about having the machine release the results of completed tests. Incorporating a "release of results sequence" feature significantly differentiated the Bio-Rad product, since most competitive instruments lacked this feature.

PARTNERSHIPS

In most industries, the days of the vertically integrated corporation are long over. Very few companies can achieve and maintain world-class status in more than a few of the elements required to provide complete customer solutions. Instead, successful companies partner with best-in-class suppliers, subcontractors, distributors, and retailers. They form total solution supply chains with a diverse and globally linked set of suppliers to satisfy equally diverse customer needs and desires. Thus, it is important to view a portfolio as the collection of solutions available from potential supply chains, not just a company's own product line.

A Coopers & Lybrand Trendsetter Barometer survey found that 56 percent of America's fastest-growing companies have partnered with others to improve existing product lines or to develop new products or services.[1] These companies take a broad view of their portfolios, leveraging their investments in new products and services by co-investing and sharing the risks and rewards with partners. Of course, these kinds of arrangements require good contracts, trust, and good faith.

Leading organizations approach their partnerships strategically by integrating them into the strategy formulation process (once the most insular and secret of all business processes). Most partners, suppliers, and providers can add much more value to a company's portfolio than just supplying manufactured parts or services—they can also have insights concerning customer value and innovative design solutions. For example, Hewlett-Packard (HP) became the world's market leader in laser printers by partnering with Canon. Canon developed and provided the printing engine, while HP used its core competencies to develop the packaging, drivers, and user interface. Dell Computer Corporation partnered with Federal Express to develop a logistics system that bypasses distributors and retailers. Using this system, Dell can operate at a negative cash flow (funded by customers and suppliers) to run a highly profitable business.[2] Cisco Systems, Inc., partnered with consultants and Web application companies to discover and develop an attribute for its networking products that is highly valued by customers: enabling customers to view and even assert some control over their entire supply chain. This customer empowerment has helped to propel Cisco to the top of its industry.

Co-investing with partners in a portfolio of customer solutions provides some big side benefits. First, it almost automatically makes the team more customer-focused by encouraging team members to expand their perspectives beyond the internal. Second, a diversity of company cultures and goals usually enhances the innovativeness and desirable attributes of the solution. Finally, all partners learn new skills and knowledge from each other.

THE BEGINNING OF THE END—OR THE END OF THE BEGINNING

By this point, any company using the MDPD process should have removed any fuzziness from the "fuzzy front end" of product development. The customer's environment and requirements should be clear. The team should understand what the customer values and what combination of features represents the best solution. Using the results of the MDPD process, the team now can begin to create a truly customer-centric product.

The final chapter of this book discusses two additional ways in which companies can enhance product definition: by using the Internet to carry out the MDPD process, and by using time to profit (rather than time to market) as a measure of product success.

12

CO-WIRED MDPD

Global Product Definition Using the Web

"This 'telephone' has too many shortcomings to be seriously considered as a means of communication."

—Western Union internal memo, 1876

NEW BUSINESS MODELS REQUIRE A NEW DEVELOPMENT MODEL

The widespread use of the Internet has accelerated the global exchange of data, voice communications, and video, and has made vast amounts of information available instantly. This communications revolution has spawned a new approach to conducting business that includes instant information exchange, virtual resource pipelines, collaborative design, online research, virtual online design, and electronic commerce (e-commerce). We refer to this new business approach as "co-wired." In a co-wired environment, as in traditional environments, people can communicate frequently, both formally and informally. Unlike the situation in a traditional environment, however, partners, suppliers, and customers may be located in different regions and even different time zones without jeopardizing the project, which can carry on via threaded discussions (in real time or not) and overlapped meetings.

The ascendance of the Internet also has created a tremendous opportunity for establishing global product definition more quickly than ever before. Once they fully understand the process, practitioners of MDPD can use Web-based tools to explore, digest, evaluate, and define what provides value to the customer. Using the Web can shorten the time needed for product definition, reduce time to market, and speed time to profit.

Since the Web is dynamic and evolving, caution and careful implementation are the watchwords. Properly applied, the Internet offers near-limitless opportunities with potentially staggering payback. This chapter explores Web-based tools and approaches that have worked well—and not so well—in the MDPD process. Finally, we offer some thoughts on speed and some research results that show that getting a product to market in the shortest amount of time does not necessarily contribute the most to company profits.

GETTING CLOSE TO CUSTOMERS, VIRTUALLY

The Internet provides an unprecedented opportunity for companies to learn about customers quickly and deeply and for development and marketing teams to learn how to think like customers. Before the Internet, Abbott Laboratories' Ross Products Division, the maker of Similac infant formula, operated "The Welcome Addition Club" to help expectant mothers prepare for their babies. The company took a traditional marketing approach, mailing information and coupons to expectant and new mothers—a useful service that resulted in some additional sales of formula and exposure for the Similac brand. Creating a Welcome Addition Club Web site[1] has taken this customer interaction to a new level. According to Miles D. White, chief executive officer of Abbott Laboratories,

> This site allows us to have an ongoing dialogue with customers, to establish relationships that go beyond the commercial, and to learn more about our customers and their feelings

about our products and their [our] competitors than we could ever have learned before. Club members tell us when they're expecting; we send them a stream of information geared to the changing state of their baby's development. The service becomes an attentive advisor to expectant mothers. . . . The result is a true win-win: we learn more about what our customer wants to know, and wants from us, and we establish a mutually beneficial relationship that ultimately leads to that customer purchasing our products, perhaps online, as she's viewing new information on the Welcome Addition Club site.[2]

Kimberly-Clark, the maker of Huggies disposable diapers and Pull-Ups training pants for toddlers, maintains a separate site for each product line that concentrates on issues important to the customers in each market segment. Similarly, the company has created sites for each major product group in its portfolio: family care (Kleenex tissue and Cottonelle bathroom tissue), adult care (Depends), feminine care (Kotex), and professional health care products. The sites are devoted to the issues and concerns of the particular customer segment and provide a basis for Kimberly-Clark to establish lifelong relationships with its customers.

Companies can use the Web to learn more about what customers value at several points in the product definition process: when gathering customer data, when prioritizing customer requirements, and when evaluating the effectiveness of potential solutions.

GATHERING CUSTOMER DATA— THE IDEAL VERSUS THE REAL

The best method of obtaining customer input will always be talking to the customer face to face in the customer's environment. However, development teams often have truncated schedules and face financial or personnel resource constraints. When development teams confront these situations, the Web offers a viable alternative to forgoing or curtailing customer input. Customers can provide video tours of their facilities. The team can conduct interviews using videoconferencing. By identifying customer requirements using remote methods, the team can rapidly identify product or service attributes that customers value.

As emphasized in Chapter 4, establishing rapport and bonding with interviewees is critical to effective communications. Developing trust is as critical in effective electronic communication as in face-to-face communication. Interviewing over the Internet limits the interviewer's ability to read body language signals; the interviewer may miss the reading-between-the-lines insights obtainable from face-to-face communication. Correctly interpreting the customers' expressed data input to ascertain the tacit information, based on facts, becomes paramount when using the Web. This may present a significant challenge, since the single biggest shortcoming of the interview process is the failure to adequately probe, and probing is made more difficult by the process of remote interviewing.

Figure 12.1 highlights the differences between executing three common communication steps in face-to-face interviews and electronically.

Figure 12.1. Three communication steps.

Communication Steps	Face-to-Face Communication	Electronic Communication
Received	Eye contact	Acknowledged pre-reading
Understood	Head nod, body language	Active listening, probing, and discussion
Acted upon	Record and observe	Report

USING THE WEB FOR DATA GATHERING

Companies can use Web-based tools to help them gather data on customer preferences, customer satisfaction, and the ranking of customer requirements. Chapter 8 discussed the efficiency of Web-based surveying. Waiting for survey results by mail and waiting for the tabulation of manual or telephone surveys can consume huge portions of the time allotted for product definition. Using Web-based survey techniques, customers can input data directly in a format readable by tabulating software, eliminating the need to reenter data. Carole Katz, director of market research and analysis at Avaya, Inc. (formerly Lucent Technologies), uses the Web to conduct Kano surveys. By doing so, Avaya reduces the typical survey cost of $50,000 to $70,000 to between $10,000 and $20,000, and cuts the time required to obtain results and analyze data in half, from four to six weeks to between two and three weeks.

USING THE WEB TO EVALUATE SOLUTIONS

The third area where the Web can help is evaluating alternative solutions. Xerox created a Web site[3] to help customers evaluate copier and finisher design features online. At the site, customers could add or subtract feature options—including stapling, C folding, Z folding, hole punching, and saddle stitching—by dragging and dropping icons. The price changed automatically with the addition or removal of each feature. The system requested a ranking of the importance of each feature and tracked the order in which the customer chose options, and also the order in which options were removed if the price got too high. Including the price associated with a given feature revealed which feature sets and price points customers valued. This allowed Xerox to understand what trade-offs engineers could consider making in relation to how customers valued the feature.

Focus is one critical factor in successfully conducting solutions selection research online. Alternative solutions must be well defined. Target markets or appropriate segments within the market must be clearly delineated. Once the team has identified a target market, it needs to create a representative panel to obtain statistically significant results. (In Xerox's case, this was 400 people, with 100 in each major market segment.) Doing this, of course, means obtaining customer names and demographics and company information. While several online companies specialize in maintaining panels, it is up to the team to validate and screen the panel to ensure that the group is representative.

All the rules of customer language discussed earlier apply to the evaluation of solutions on the Web. "Engineeringese" needs to be translated into language that customers can understand and relate to. The team must address the issues that arise when survey respondents are of different nationalities and cultures and speak different languages (which may happen more often when a company uses the Web for surveying).

There is a substantial startup cost to using the Web for solution evaluation (building market panels, prototyping evaluation software, setting up logistics), but the potential payoff can be worth the investment. By putting in the effort up front to get a quality panel in the proper target markets, Xerox reduced the time to market acceptance and increased engineering effectiveness. Engineers could get the panel's feedback and resolve a problem within a week—a time frame unheard of using traditional market research approaches.

Development teams must also consider the impact of the Web-based solution survey on potential customers. Virtual reality can sometimes eclipse the real world, so keeping the presentation as close to the real world as possible is important. For example, if you were developing a car jack, you could create a site similar to the Xerox site that showed the attributes of the jack and let the customer build the jack virtually. You could test the customer designs (again virtually) to predict how one product would be valued versus another. In doing so, however, you would need to pay careful attention to how the Web experience might set customer expectations. If you create the impression that the product will use a more rugged material than the material you plan to use for manufacturing, you may risk disappointing customers and potentially failing in the marketplace.

DEVELOPING A CUSTOMER DATABASE

Collecting customer data via the Internet often brings up the issue of knowledge management. Gathering and using customer data effectively across a geographically dispersed organization requires the development of a database that developers and marketing staff in remote locations can access via the Web. The first step in accomplishing this is to put the data online and make them available to the teams that are generating the information. Carole Katz from Avaya has completed eighteen projects using VOC, a modified MDPD process. During all those projects, every project team's work, including all the image and requirement diagrams, was saved in a database that her team could access. A project with a global scope might generate 700 or 800 requirements, of which about thirty make it to the final requirements diagram. "That doesn't mean the 700 remaining balance aren't valid," Katz says. "They just may not have been the ones the team felt were the most compelling given the team's particular challenge. We have now entered all that into a database and can slice, dice, and sort on key words for any given question around customer requirements that comes up in the business. We can go into the database and generate results for teams looking at requirements for development or images for advertising and message content. We are able to do those kinds of searches in a matter of hours; otherwise they would have taken us days, maybe weeks, or we would have just lost the information."

By adapting the MDPD process, Avaya reduced the time required for projects and allowed its project teams to leapfrog or short-circuit some of the steps in the process. As companies make the transition to customer-centric product definition, developing an accessible Web-based customer knowledge database increases the opportunity for remote offices and facilities to understand the customer and the products being developed.

REMOTE COLLABORATION

Web-based collaboration tools can accelerate the product definition process by condensing the time required for particular stages of MDPD. Product definition teams can brainstorm solutions using virtual meeting software, 3-D modeling tools, or collaborative whiteboard applications and can present solutions to customers and receive input at Internet speed. (The sidebar on page 184 lists various types of Web-based tools for collaboration.)

Using traditional techniques, an MDPD project typically takes twelve to sixteen weeks. Customer visits, surveying, and analyzing alternative solutions typically consume the greatest amount of time. Figure 12.2 shows where Web-based tools can save time, potentially reducing the schedule to nine weeks.

Using the Web for MDPD has several advantages. As we have mentioned, reduced time and cost are the greatest benefits. Customers may be located in different regions and even different time zones. Web-based tools simplify scheduling and mitigate the effect of time zone differences, since the interviewer (in one time zone) does not necessarily have to be available at the same time as the interviewee (in another time zone). This can save weeks when a team is researching international markets. Similarly, teams can brainstorm and quickly validate and modify ideas in real time using whiteboards and collaboration tools. Using Web-based collaboration tools also results in more structured communications. Since there are no opportunities for informal exchanges, all communication is traceable and can be indexed. This means that knowledge is immediately transferred and visible, well managed, and shared within the development team and by customers.

There are also potential problems associated with making the Web part of the MDPD process. Web-based interviewing reduces the team's ability to truly empathize with customers. Obtaining contextual data, even with a video, is very difficult. This increases the risk of missing a "wow" requirement—a need that customers don't or can't articulate, but that becomes obvious during an in-person interview.

Web-based surveys outside the United States may be constrained

Figure 12.2. Web collaboration tools speed the process.

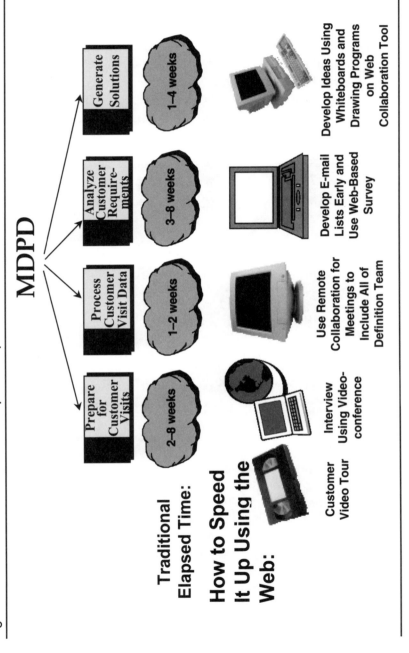

by the slower rate of Internet adoption in Europe and the Asia-Pacific region. Companies must take care that survey participants accurately represent market segments for the potential solution. Finally, collaborative tools are still in their infancy, as is the technology that drives them. As the technology matures, using it will get easier, but in the meantime, teams must deal with frustrations such as software programs that crash, slow Internet connections, and tools that are less than intuitive to use.

Web Tools for Collaboration

The categories of Web tools that can facilitate product definition work are still evolving. Tools usually fall into one of the following groups, with overlap among some of the groups in terms of features and capabilities.

1. Virtual meeting
   - Enables conducting online business conversations with anyone, anytime, across geographic and organizational boundaries for conferences and meetings
   - Has varying levels of security, features, and prices
   - Enables cooperative group document creation, editing, and publishing
   - Allows digital signing of documents with a guaranteed audit trail
2. Knowledge collaboration
   - Can assemble, organize, distribute, and share information
   - Can turn disconnected pieces of information into a coherent visual framework
   - Can provide multilingual capabilities
3. Knowledge management
   - Makes available content management, information sharing, workflow, and publishing software
   - Provides artificial intelligence and fuzzy logic that deepen the user's understanding of commercial and practical issues affecting an important decision

- Enables organizations to capture and store knowledge
- Enables users to access and retrieve knowledge through natural language queries and neural network technology
- Automatically discovers the knowledge, expertise, and interests of users
4. File sharing
- Enables the managing and sharing of information about projects with clients, co-workers, customers, and suppliers
5. Search
- Allows users to organize Web searches and share them with friends and co-workers

TIME TO MARKET OR TIME TO PROFIT?

Web-based tools speed the research process and undoubtedly will become more central to research and product definition. Yet, regardless of the research tools or methods of communication used, the fundamental purpose of the MDPD process is to discover those customer requirements that lead to solutions that *differentiate* a product or service in its market. After the buzz about the Web has subsided, the real battle in the marketplace will continue. Market size, market share, first mover advantage, and market dominance all begin with identifying requirements and creating products with long-term product differentiation. Learning how to identify and satisfy customer needs in a way that leads to product differentiation and profit is the payback for a company's investment of time and resources in the MDPD process.

Many organizations press for rapid programs to release products to market more quickly, believing that this is in the best interest of the bottom line. Short-term programs, however, have a relatively long time to profit, even though their development costs are modest—a fact that seems counterintuitive. Trying to shorten development time by adding incremental products developed off an existing product platform may backfire unless the products are truly differentiated in the marketplace.

In fact, a PDC benchmarking study[4] found that *longer product development programs have more rapid payback*. Short-term programs (those with about a six-month time to market) typically involve incremental variants of existing products that are intended to fill out a product line. The availability of Web-based tools makes it seem easy to get a "quick read" on the market, but there are no shortcuts to creating a product with real points of difference and long-term market potential.

At the other extreme, *very long* development projects have a very long time to profit. Sometimes they never pay back; sometimes they pay back in a major way, but it takes a long time because of the large investment required. However, projects that fall in the middle in terms of time to market have the fastest time to profit. These products have just the right amount of innovation and cycle time and command a relatively higher margin. Customers place great value on points of product differentiation that have been identified using the MDPD process. Selecting the optimum project based on points of differentiation is the key. The greater the degree of difference, the larger the profit. The chart in Figure 12.3 shows a J-curve relationship between time to market and time to profit. This suggests that it is better to strive for the shortest time to

Figure 12.3. Time to market versus time to profit.

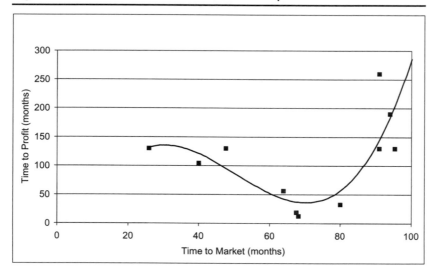

market differentiation, even if this means a relatively longer time to market.

FOLLOW THE CUSTOMER, FOLLOW THE MONEY

Too often, companies make product portfolio decisions by looking at internal variables like risk, time to market, or whether the product leverages a previously developed platform. This is misguided because customers don't pay for things like leveraged platforms. They pay for innovative, complete solutions—not me-too products where competition is high and margins are thin. Companies should make product decisions by assessing the degree of differentiation and how well the product meets the customers' requirements compared to the investment, not by looking at time to market or market risk versus technical risk charts.

Products with a shorter time to profit may require a greater investment of time and money. For these products, it is essential that the product definition satisfies customer requirements and creates truly identifiable points of differentiation. Defining these products is the essence of MDPD. Yet when companies use time to market as the criterion for investigating potential new product development projects, they often foreshorten (or forgo altogether) the up-front product definition process.

In the typical economic product life cycle (Figure 12.4), the major expenditure occurs in the development phase. Not only is the investigation phase much shorter in duration, but also significantly less is expended in this phase. Yet this is when companies make crucial decisions about project selection, allocate R&D funds, and configure teams. Is it any wonder that the term *fuzzy front end* has become ingrained in the development process? In Figure 12.4, the darkly shaded area represents the ideal expenditure in the investigative phase in light of the disparity between time to market and time to profit.

The MDPD process is a robust and thorough method of uncovering the expressed and, more important, unexpressed or latent desires and needs of the customer. It provides a detailed framework and develops factual criteria for evaluating new products (and competitors' products)

Figure 12.4. Economics of the product life cycle (COGS is cost of goods sold).

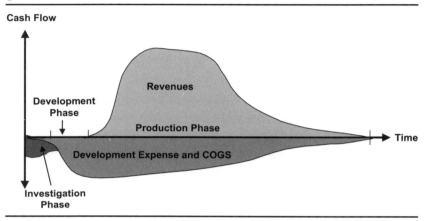

against customer requirements. The MDPD process has been demonstrated and documented to transcend the boundaries of product development, influencing all functions within the business organization, from marketing and manufacturing to distribution and finance. The process begins with the customer. It allows the development team to deeply empathize with the customers and lets *what the customer values* drive the organization to develop the right products, at the right time, for the right price, in the right place.

Appendix

This appendix shows the flow of the MDPD process from beginning to end, as well as the relationships among all the diagrams and documents referred to in the book. This overview should help the reader create a mental image of the process and provide a thorough understanding of how all the pieces fit together.

We chose a golf bag for our example, since golf is a sport that is growing worldwide and is probably appreciated—and played—by many readers. (Also, I love the game!) More important, this example vividly illustrates the relationships of all the elements in the MDPD process. The interviews and survey data were readily available from golfing buddies, friends, relatives, and associates with golfing experience, and were compiled easily using the Web. We didn't scientifically validate the study results, since they were intended merely to provide a road map through the process, not to actually design a new golf bag.

The documents included in the appendix are

- Customer matrix
- Image diagram
- Requirements diagram
- Initial golf bag survey
- Self-stated importance results
- Reflected sum of the rank scores
- Kano results and chart

- Competitive matrix
- Requirements and solutions matrix

THE CUSTOMER MATRIX AND INTERVIEWS

The first step in implementing the MDPD process to design a new golf bag was to develop a representative sample of potential customers. We constructed the customer matrix to provide a geographically diverse cross section of participants: lead users, users with low to high golf handicaps, both sexes, various ages, and various income levels. We did not consider frequency of play because differences in *use* did not surface between recreational golfers and avid ones. The resulting customer matrix is shown in Figure A.1.

THE IMAGE DIAGRAM

The next step in the process involved interviewing the golfers in their contextual setting: on and near the golf course. This was the fun part! We conducted telephone interviews when logistics prevented actual visits. Then again, talking about golf can be almost as enjoyable as playing it. We collected hundreds of images and concepts from the transcripts. As the collection process continued, we experienced the law of diminishing returns. When new opportunities stopped appearing, we stopped interviewing. We then extracted the images from the transcripts and narrowed them to the vital few using the digestion method. We then combined these vital few using the language analysis tool to create the image diagram shown in Figure A.2.

THE REQUIREMENTS DIAGRAM

These images centered on the golfers' frustration that the golf bag got in their way instead of being an asset. Clearly, golfers desire the removal of all obstacles to playing better golf.

Figure A.1. The customer matrix.

Household Name	# of interviews:	Male (All)	Female (All)	U.S. West Coast (3)	U.S. SE (3)	U.S. MW (3)	U.S. NE (3)	Australia (3)	Japan (3)	Spain (3)	England (3)	<10 (5)	10-20 (5)	20-55 (5)	>55 (5)	Wilson (5)	Titleist (5)	Taylor Made (5)	Ping (5)	Callaway (5)	No (5)	Yes (5)	<15 (3)	15-30 (3)	>30 (3)	>$150K (3)	$75K-$150K (3)	<$75K (3)
1 Smith		1	1				1							1					1	1	1	1	1			1		1
2 Cohn		1				1								1				1	1		1		1		1	1		
3 Greene		1	1			1									1		1	1			1			1			1	
4 Leone		1	1				1			1				1				1				1	1			1		
5 DeBiasi		1	1				1				1				1						1				1			1
6 Stuart		1						1							1	1					1			1		1		
7 Taylor		1	1	1								1	1	1			1			1		1	1					1
8 Carter		1	1		1								1	1				1		1	1		1					1
9 Abott		1	1			1				1					1			1				1		1		1		
10 Clark		1				1								1		1			1		1		1				1	
11 Norton		1											1	1			1	1			1		1					1
12 McCafferty		1	1	1	1									1	1		1		1		1			1		1		1
13 Macabe		1			1																1							
14 Springer		1	1						1				1	1	1	1		1	1		1		1			1	1	
15 Piperato		1													1		1				1		1					
16 Naguchi		1	1						1	1				1			1	1	1	1	1	1	1			1	1	
17 Santos		1													1						1			1				1
18 Collins		1									1		1		1						1		1			1		
19 Morita		1	1									1	1	1	1	1	1	1		1	1		1				1	
20 Santyana		1								1	1		1			1			1	1	1			1				1
21 Fields		1	1					1											1		1			1		1		
22 Montgomery		1		1										1		1	1			1		1	1				1	
23 Arnold		1	1		1								1	1		1	1	1			1			1				1
24 Pipen		1	1	1									1	1	1	1	1	1		1	1		1		1	1	1	1
TOTALS		23	11	3	3	3	3	3	3	3	3	2	5	9	8	5	5	4	4	5	18	6	9	9	6	7	9	6
NET				0	0	0	0	0	0	0	0	-3	0	4	3	0	0	-1	-1	0	13	1	6	6	3	4	6	3

191

Figure A.2. The image diagram.

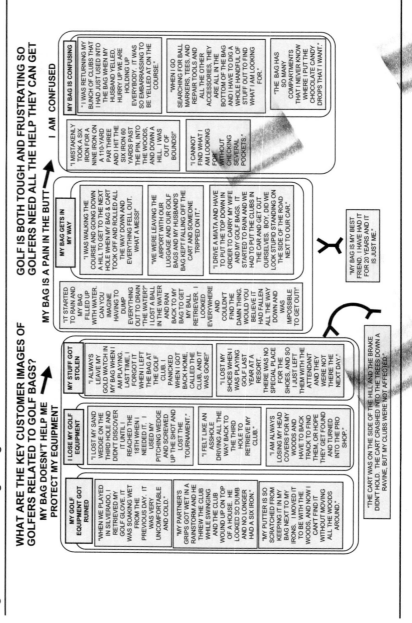

Using the image diagram and transcripts, we next created customer requirements statements. This was our opportunity to expand beyond what the interviewees had actually said and come up with some of the "wows" by using the images to expand our thought process. One theme that emerged during this study was that the golfers wanted their bags to be an asset to their game. The last thing a golfer wants to contend with when looking for a new ball, putting a club away, or finding an accessory after hitting an errant shot is an unfriendly golf bag. The requirements diagram in Figure A.3 lists the requirements that emerged from the application of the translation process.

METRICS

Once the requirements were identified, we developed metrics to measure the requirements to remove any remaining ambiguity. We defined a metric for each requirement to ensure that potential solutions would meet the requirement. For example:

Customer Requirement # 7: You can return your club to the bag quickly.

Metric for Customer Requirement # 7: Measure the amount of time that it takes to return any one club to the golf bag.

Operational Definition: Select a representative set of people across the categories of the customer matrix. Have each person, one at a time, without any of the others watching, execute the steps below:

1. Remove a club from the bag.
2. Wait five minutes (to minimize the impact of knowing where you took it from).
3. Start the timer when the person is next to the bag.
4. Put the club back in the bag.
5. When the club is back in the bag, stop the timer.
6. Check to make sure that the club is in the proper place.
7. If yes, record the score. If no, continue the timer till yes.
8. Repeat for each of the fourteen clubs carried in a golf bag.

Figure A.3. The requirements diagram.

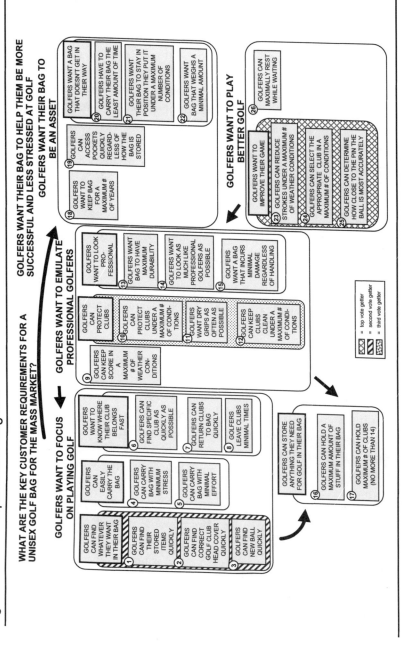

THE SURVEY

It was now time to get feedback from the customer to determine how the customer prioritized the requirements. The surveys, as earlier mentioned, were conducted via e-mail, and the entire process was completed in days. Figure A.4 shows the actual survey used.

THE SURVEY RESULTS

Armed with the data from the completed surveys, we developed the RSOR scores and plotted the Kano data. We expanded the requirements diagram to incorporate the IBT (if-better-than) and IWT (if-worse-than) scores identified in the Kano survey. Recall that the IBT is the combined score of attractive and one-dimensional requirements, and IWT is the combination of must-be and one-dimensional requirements. Figures A.5, A.6, A.7, and A.8 show the resulting output.

If you examine the results for requirement 23, "golfer wants to reduce the number of strokes regardless of the weather," you find a strongly attractive score on the Kano (IBT = 100 and IWT = 38), a very high importance score (more than 80 percent rated it extremely important or very important), and a medium RSOR score (21). If we hadn't done the Kano survey, the assumption would be that requirement number 23 is important, and that therefore we need to better our competition on this. But with the Kano IWT score of 38, we don't lose many points by not doing this. If we do it, it will be a "wow" and we can focus our PR campaign around the golfer protecting his clubs. We decided not to solve this one and to focus our R&D dollars on other requirements. We wouldn't have known that we could do this if we hadn't analyzed the Kano data.

Once we analyzed the results of the survey, we could use the IBT and IWT scores as weighting factors for an analysis of our competitors. We undertook an analysis of competitive bags to determine the best-in-class of competitive existing solutions. We selected three brands, Calla-

Figure A.4. The survey.

SECTION A

For each of the following questions, please mark the number corresponding to the appropriate response to the right of the question.

1. Indicate which best represents your USGA handicap. ___
 	
    Less than 15 (1)
    Between 15 and 30 (2)
    Greater than 30 (3)
    No USGA handicap (4)
	2. Specify the bracket describing your age group. ___
	
	    Younger than 19 (1)
	    Greater than 19 and less than 39 (2)
	    Greater than 39 and less than 55 (3)
	    Greater than 55 (4)

3. Select the golf bag you are currently using (if more than one, select the one you use most frequently). ___
 	
    Callaway (1)
    Ping (2)
    Taylor Made (3)
    Titleist (4)
    Wilson (5)
    Other (6) Please specify ___
	4. Indicate your gender. ___
	
	    Male (1)
	    Female (2)

5. Indicate that which best represents the manner in which you play golf most frequently. ___
 	
    Ride using a golf cart (1)
    Walk using a hand cart (2)
    Walk carrying bag (3)	

SECTION B - Instruction

For each of the following questions, you should ask, "How important would it be if . . . ," then complete the sentence based on the requirement listed in the first column. For the example provided below, the question would read, "How important would it be if you had more places to hold cups in your car?"

You would then place the corresponding code number (e.g., 1 for "not at all important," 2 for "somewhat important," etc.) in the appropriate box in that column. The last column on the right (titled "ranking") is used to rank those requirements that the respondent indicates are "extremely important." For all those requirements rated as "extremely important," rank in order their *relative* importance in the right-hand column, designating the most important as "1," the next most important as "2," etc.

Note: In this example, the respondent chose both requirement 1 and requirement 3 as "extremely important," which is marked with the number "5." He then ranked requirement 3 as the *most important,* and requirement 1 as the *next most important.*

Requirement *How important would it be if:*	1 = **Not at All Important** 2 = **Somewhat Important** 3 = **Important** 4 = **Very Important** 5 = **Extremely Important**	*Ranking*
1. You had more places to hold cups in your car?	5	2
2. You could hold different size cups in your car?	2	
3. You could access your drink in you car from several positions?	5	1

PLEASE DO NOT FORGET TO RANK-ORDER AT LEAST YOUR FIRST THREE EXTREMELY IMPORTANT RESPONSES.

(continued)

Figure A.4. (cont.)

SECTION B - Questions

Requirement *How important would it be if:*	1 = Not at All Important 2 = Somewhat Important 3 = Important 4 = Very Important 5 = Extremely Important	*Ranking*
1. You could find the items that you have stored in the bag quickly?		
2. You could find the correct golf club head cover quickly?		
3. You could find a new ball quickly?		
4. You could carry your bag with little stress?		
5. You could carry your bag with little effort?		
6. You could quickly find a specific club?		
7. You could quickly return your club to the bag?		
8. You left your clubs behind at a prior hole fewer times?		
9. You could keep score easily regardless of the weather?		
10. You could protect your clubs regardless of the weather conditions?		
11. You could more frequently have dry grips (even in humid or wet weather)?		
12. You could keep your clubs clean?		
13. You had a bag that lasted a long time?		
14. You looked like a professional golfer?		
15. You had a bag that didn't get damaged regardless of how it was handled?		
16. You could hold a lot of stuff in your bag?		
17. You could hold as many as fourteen clubs in your bag?		
18. You could keep your bag for many years?		
19. You could get at the bag's pockets regardless of how the bag was stored?		
20. You infrequently had to carry your bag?		
21. Your bag would stay in the position you put it?		
22. Your bag weighed less?		
23. You could reduce your number of strokes regardless of the weather?		
24. You could select the appropriate club?		
25. You could determine the distance the ball was from the flag on the green?		
26. You could rest while waiting?		

SECTION C - Instruction

The following are pairs of multiple-choice questions about potential product capabilities. The first question in each pair asks how you would feel if the product included a particular capability to an extent greater than you have that capability today; the second question in each pair asks how you would feel if you had less of that capability than you have today.

You should place an **X** in the column that corresponds with your answer to each question. The cup holder example shown below demonstrates how one customer might answer such pairs of questions. For example, for question 1a, the respondent would expect that he would have more places to hold cups in their car than he has today. The customer's answer is marked with an **X** in the second column. The second question, 2a, asks how the customer would feel if there were a variety of cup type options, and question 2b asks how the customer would feel if the options were limited. The customer's response is indicated with an **X** in "1" and "4," respectively.

It is critical to our survey results that both the (a) and (b) parts of each question are answered.

	I would be delighted to find it that way (1)	I expect it to be that way (2)	I am neutral (3)	I would not like it that way, but I can live with it that way (4)	It must not be that way (5)
1a. If you had more places to hold cups in your car than you do today, how would you feel?		X			
1b. If you had fewer places to hold cups, how would you feel?					X
2a. If you could hold more sizes of cups in your cup holders than you can today, how would you feel?	X				
2b. If you could hold a more limited selection of cups than you can today, how would you feel?				X	

(continued)

Figure A.4. (cont.)

SECTION C - Questions

How would you feel if	I would be delighted to find it that way (1)	I expect it to be that way (2)	I am neutral (3)	I would not like it that way, but I can live with it that way (4)	It must not be that way (5)
1a. You could find items stored in your bag more quickly than today?					
1b. It took you longer to find your things?					
2a. You could find the correct golf club head cover faster than you can today?					
2b. It took you longer than it does today?					
3a. You could find a new ball in your bag more quickly than you can today?					
3b. It took you longer than it does today?					
4a. You could carry your bag with less physical stress than you can today?					
4b. You had greater stress carrying your bag than you do today?					
5a. You could carry your bag with less effort than you can today?					
5b. It took more effort than it does today?					
6a. You could find a specific club in your bag faster than you can today?					
6b. It took you longer than it does today?					
7a. You could return your clubs to your bag faster than you can today?					
7b. It took you longer to return your clubs than it does today?					
8a. You left your clubs behind less frequently than you do today?					
8b. You left you clubs behind as much as you do today?					
9a. You could keep your golf score easily in more weather conditions than you can today?					
9b. You could keep your golf score the same as you do today?					

10a. You could protect your clubs under more situations (such as rain, dust, etc.) than you can today?				
10b. You could protect your clubs in fewer situations than you can today?				
11a. You could have dry grips more frequently than you do today?				
11b. Your grips stayed the same as they are today?				
12a. You could keep your clubs clean more often than you can today?				
12b. You could keep you clubs clean less often than you can today?				
13a. Your bag was more durable than it is today?				
13b. Your bag was less durable than it is today?				
14a. You could look like a professional golfer more than you do today?				
14b. You could look like a professional golfer less often than you do today?				
15a. Your bag was damaged less than it is today regardless of how it was handled?				
15b. Your bag was damaged more than today when it was handled?				
16a. You could hold more stuff in your bag than you can today?				
16b. You could hold less stuff than you can today?				
17a. You could hold more clubs in your bag than you can today?				
17b. You could hold fewer clubs than you can today?				
18a. You could keep your bag for more years than you can today?				
18b. You could only keep your bag for fewer years than today?				
19a. You could access your pockets in the bag more quickly than you can today regardless of how the bag is stored?				
19b. It took you longer to access your pockets than it does today?				
20a. You had to carry your bag less time than you do today?				
20b. You had to carry your bag more time?				

(continued)

Figure A.4. (cont.)

How would you feel if	I would be delighted to find it that way (1)	I expect it to be that way (2)	I am neutral (3)	I would not like it that way, but I can live with it that way (4)	It must not be that way (5)
21a. Your bag stayed in the same position you placed it under more situations than it does today?					
21b. Your bag stayed in place in fewer conditions than today?					
22a. Your bag weiged less than it does today?					
22b. Your bag weighed more than today?					
23a. You could reduce your strokes under more weather conditions than you can today?					
23b. You could reduce your strokes under fewer weather conditions than you can today?					
24a. You could select the appropriate club more frequently than you can today?					
24b. There were fewer times when you could select the appropriate club?					
25a. You could rest more frequently while waiting than you can today?					
25b. You could not rest more than you can today?					

Thank you for filling in our survey. We appreciate your investing the time to help us develop products that will meet your needs.

Figure A.5. Self-stated importance results.

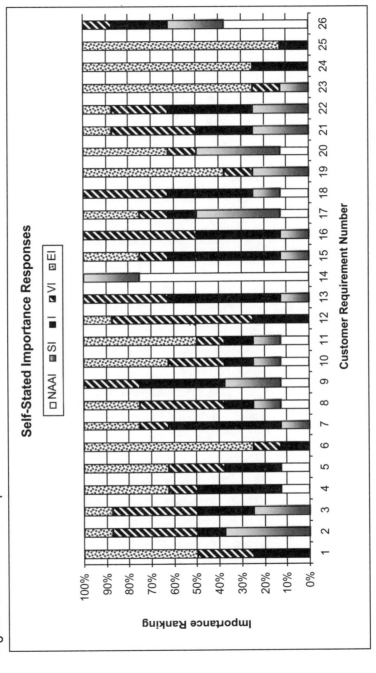

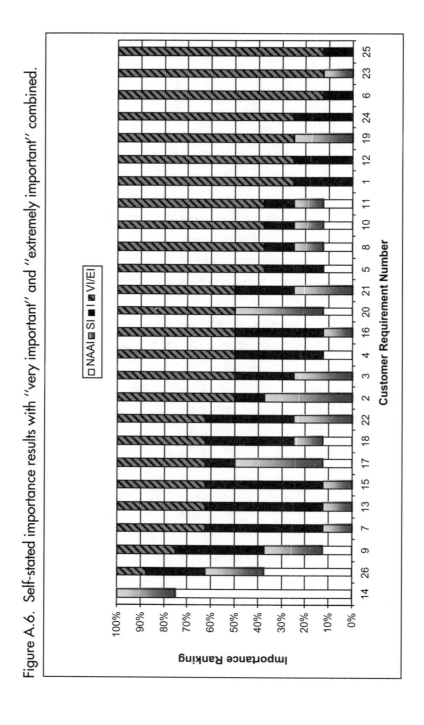

Figure A.6. Self-stated importance results with "very important" and "extremely important" combined.

Figure A.7. Reflected sum of the rank.

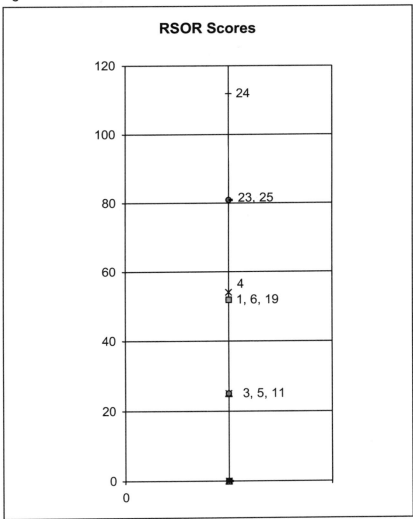

way, Ping, and Wilson, from the competition for illustration purposes only. If this had been a real undertaking, we would have included several additional competitors. Figure A.9 shows the results of this analysis and includes the weighted results. Note the last column, entitled "What to Do?" This is where we decided how we wanted to handle each of the

Figure A.8. Kano results.

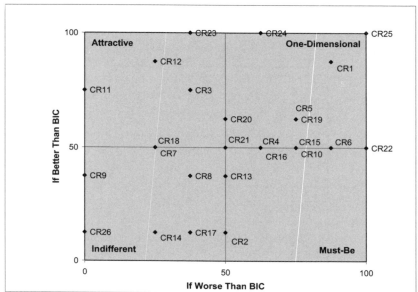

requirements based on the survey scores and the competitive positioning. We effectively decided how to apply our precious R&D dollars. This also became the basis of our PR campaign and marketing commercialization of the product.

IDEA GENERATION

In the idea generation and brainstorming step, the development team begins defining what requirements will differentiate the final product in the marketplace. At this point, we had identified best-in-class existing solutions and articulated the customer requirements. We next had to select the attributes of the new golf bag that best satisfy the requirements. Figures A.10*a* and *b* give examples of the type of idea generation we undertook when brainstorming solutions.

After we brainstormed ideas for each requirement, we combined

Figure A.9. The competitive matrix.

REQUIREMENT		#	Survey Results			Best in Class (BIC)	Existing Solution Callaway		Existing Solution Wilson		Existing Solution Ping		What To Do?
			RSOR	IBT	IWT		RAW	WGT	RAW	WGT	RAW	WGT	
Golfer wants to focus on playing golf	Golfers can find whatever is needed in their bag												
		Find item in the bag quickly	1	52	88	88	Ping	-1	-88	-1	-88	0	0	Better than BIC
		Find correct golf club head cover quickly	2	0	13	50	Callaway	0	0	0	0	0	0	Meet BIC
		Find a new ball quickly	3	25	75	38	Callaway	0	0	-1	-38	-1	-38	Wow
	Golfer can easily carry the bag	Carry your bag with little stress	4	54	50	63	Ping	-1	-63	-1	-63	0	0	Better than BIC
		Carry your bag with little effort	5	25	63	75	Ping	-1	-75	-1	-75	0	0	Better than BIC
	Golfer wants to know where their club belongs fast	Quickly find a specific club	6	52	50	88	Wilson	-1	-88	0	0	-1	-88	Better than BIC
		Quickly return your club to the bag	7	0	50	25	Wilson	-1	-25	0	0	-1	-25	As well as BIC
		You left your clubs behind at a prior hole fewer times	8	0	38	38	none	-1	-38	-1	-38	-1	-38	Nothing
Golfer wants to emulate a professional golfer	Keep score easily regardless of the weather		9	0	38	0	none	-1	0	-1	0	-1	0	Nothing
	Golfer can protect his clubs	Protect your clubs regardless of the weather conditions	10	0	50	75	Ping	-1	-75	-1	-75	0	0	As well as BIC
		Have dry grips	11	25	75	0	none	-1	0	-1	0	-1	0	Wow
		Keep your clubs clean	12	0	88	25	none	-1	-25	-1	-25	-1	-25	Wow
	Golfer wants to look professional	Bag that lasted a long time	13	0	38	50	Callaway	0	0	-1	-50	-1	-50	Be Competitive
		Looked like a professional golfer	14	0	13	25	Ping	-1	-25	-1	-25	0	0	Nothing
		Bag that didn't get damaged regardless of how handled	15	0	50	75	none	-1	-75	-1	-75	-1	-75	As well as BIC
Golfer wants to store anything they need for golf in their bag		Hold a lot of stuff in your bag	16	0	50	63	Ping	-1	-63	-1	-63	0	0	As well as BIC
		Hold as many as fourteen clubs in your bag	17	0	13	38	None	0	0	0	0	0	0	Nothing
Golfer wants the bag to be an asset	Keep your bag for many years		18	0	50	25	Ping	-1	-25	-1	-25	0	0	Nothing
		Get at bag's pockets regardless of how bag stored	19	52	63	75	Ping	-1	-75	-1	-75	0	0	Better than BIC
	Golfer wants a bag that doesn't get in the way	Infrequently had to carry your bag	20	0	63	50	None	-1	-50	-1	-50	-1	-50	As well as BIC
		Bag stays in position you put it	21	0	50	50	Callaway	0	0	-1	-50	-1	-50	As well as BIC
		Bag weighs less	22	0	50	100	Ping	-1	-100	-1	-100	0	0	As well as BIC
Golfer wants to play better golf	Golfer wants to improve his game	Reduce your number of strokes regardless of the weather	23	81	100	38	None	-1	-38	-1	-38	-1	-38	Nothing
		Select the appropriate club	24	112	100	63	Ping	-1	-63	-1	-63	0	0	Wow
		Determine the distance the ball was from the flag on the green	25	81	100	100	None	-1	-100	-1	-100	-1	-100	Better than BIC
		Could rest while waiting	26	0	13	0	None	-1	0	-1	0	-1	0	Nothing
									-1088		-1113		-575	

the best of each requirement's ideas together to form three different solutions.

The following are the features of New Solution A:

- The bag is rectangular (there are pockets on three sides for easy access when the bag is on the golf cart).

Figure A.10a. Potential solutions.

Validity	Feasibility	**Customer Requirement # 7: You can quickly return your club to your bag**
H	H	(1) Separate place for each club
H	H	(2) Angle to create steps
L		(3) Dividers are foam
M	H	(4) Number the slots
H	H	(5) External putter holder
H	H	(6) Clubs all on outside with a swivel base

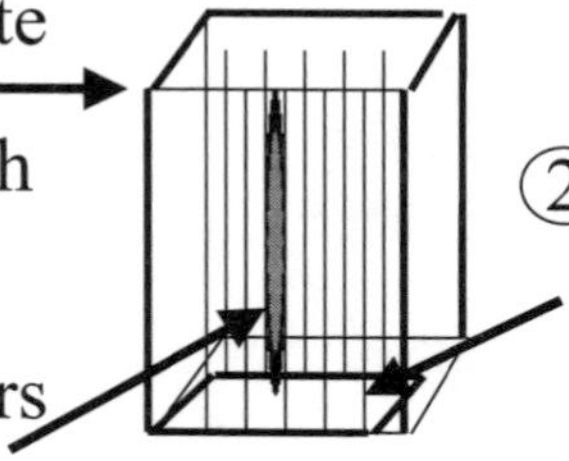

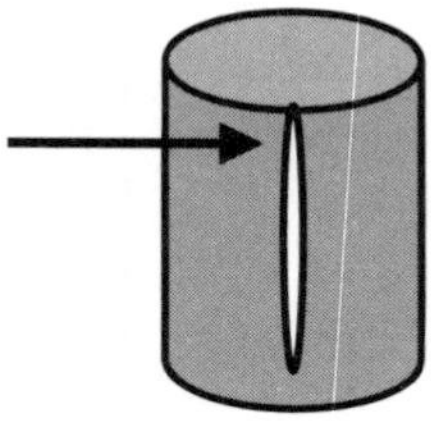

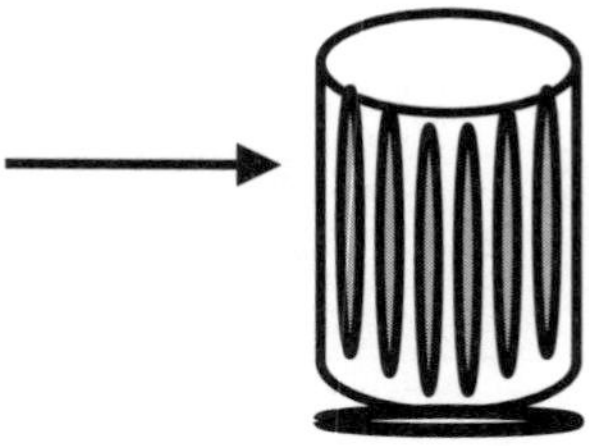

Figure A.10b. Potential solutions.

Validity	Feasibility	**Customer Requirement # 7:** **You can quickly return your club to your bag**
H	H	⑦Long balloons to hold the clubs 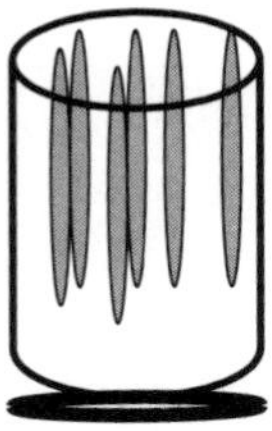
H	M	⑧Slot opens for correct club Scanner 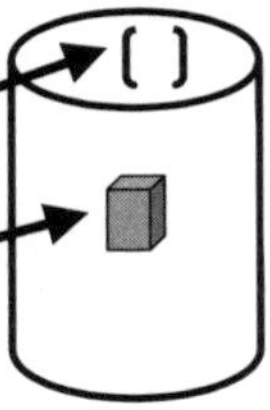
H	H	⑨ Turnstile for clubs ⑩Scanner 

- There are individual fastenings on the bag for head covers to attach to (to prevent loss).

- There is a small personal digital assistant to collect and display club usage per distance, record scores, and putts (play better golf).

- There is a tube for each club to maintain separation for easy entry and exit (prevent club grips from crossing and tangling in bag).

- Each tube is identified with the club number (quickly identify clubs and missing ones).

- Tubes are made out of absorbent or chamois cloth (keep grips dry).

- A tag on each zipper identifies what goes in which compartment (organize equipment).

- Zippers on pockets open on three sides like a rollout tray to enable greater visibility of inside without stuff falling out (quick access to everything in bag).

- There is an external ball and tee dispenser (ease of access to balls and tees).

- There is an external club head cleaner (clubs clean).

- There is an easily retractable rain cover to protect clubs (protect clubs).

- There are wheels for rolling as opposed to lifting bag (carry bag with less stress).

EVALUATING SOLUTIONS

We evaluated each solution by expanding the competitive matrix to include the new concepts A, B, and C, as shown in Figure A.11.

Solutions A, B, and C address different requirements and assume different levels of investment, technical and manufacturing risk, resource capabilities, and schedules—in essence, the business case for each is dif-

Figure A.11. Requirements and solutions matrix.

REQUIREMENT	#	Survey Results			Best in Class (BIC)	Existing Solution Callaway		Existing Solution Wilson		Existing Solution Ping		What To Do?	New Solution A		New Solution B		New Solution C	
		RSOR	IBT	IWT		RAW	WGT	RAW	WGT	RAW	WGT		RAW	WGT	RAW	WGT	RAW	WGT
Find item in the bag quickly	1	52	88	88	Ping	-1	-88	-1	-88	0	0	Better than BIC	1	88	0	0	1	0
Find correct golf club head cover quickly	2	0	13	50	Callaway	0	0	0	0	0	0	Meet BIC	0	0	0	0	0	0
Find a new ball quickly	3	25	75	38	Callaway	0	0	-1	-38	-1	-38	Wow	1	75	1	75	1	75
Carry your bag with little stress	4	54	50	63	Ping	-1	-63	-1	-63	0	0	Better than BIC	0	0	0	0	0	0
Carry your bag with little effort	5	25	63	75	Ping	-1	-75	-1	-75	0	0	Better than BIC	0	0	0	0	0	0
Quickly find a specific club	6	52	50	88	Wilson	-1	-88	0	0	-1	-88	Better than BIC	1	50	1	50	1	50
Quickly return your club to the bag	7	0	50	25	Wilson	-1	-25	0	0	-1	-25	As well as BIC	1	50	1	50	1	50
You left your clubs behind at a prior hole fewer times	8	0	38	38	none	-1	-38	-1	-38	-1	-38	Nothing	0	0	0	0	0	0
Keep score easily regardless of the weather	9	0	38	0	none	-1	0	-1	0	-1	0	Nothing	0	0	0	0	0	0
Protect your clubs regardless of the weather conditions	10	0	50	75	Ping	-1	-75	-1	-75	0	0	As well as BIC	0	0	0	0	0	0
Have dry grips	11	25	75	0	none	-1	0	-1	0	-1	0	Wow	1	75	0	0	0	0
Keep your clubs clean	12	0	88	25	none	-1	-25	-1	-25	-1	-25	Wow	1	88	0	0	1	88
Bag that lasted a long time	13	0	38	50	Callaway	0	0	-1	-50	-1	-50	Be Competitive	0	0	0	0	0	0
Looked like a professional golfer	14	0	13	25	Ping	-1	-25	-1	-25	0	0	Nothing	0	0	0	0	0	0
Bag that didn't get damaged regardless of how handled	15	0	50	75	none	-1	-75	-1	-75	-1	-75	As well as BIC	0	0	0	0	0	0
Hold a lot of stuff in your bag	16	0	50	63	Ping	-1	-63	-1	-63	0	0	As well as BIC	1	50	0	0	0	0
Hold as many as fourteen clubs in your bag	17	0	13	38	None	0	0	0	0	0	0	Nothing	0	0	0	0	0	0
Keep your bag for many years	18	0	50	25	Ping	-1	-25	-1	-25	0	0	Nothing	-1	-25	-1	-25	-1	-25
Get at bag's pockets regardless of how bag stored	19	52	63	75	Ping	-1	-75	-1	-75	0	0	Better than BIC	1	63	1	63	0	0
Infrequently had to carry your bag	20	0	63	50	None	-1	-50	-1	-50	-1	-50	As well as BIC	0	0	1	63	0	0
Bag stays in position you put it	21	0	50	50	Callaway	0	0	-1	-50	-1	-50	As well as BIC	1	50	1	50	0	0
Bag weighs less	22	0	50	100	Ping	-1	-100	-1	-100	0	0	As well as BIC	0	0	-1	-100	0	0
Reduce your number of strokes regardless of the weather	23	81	100	38	None	-1	-38	-1	-38	-1	-38	Nothing	-1	-38	-1	-38	-1	-38
Select the appropriate club	24	112	100	63	Ping	-1	-63	-1	-63	0	0	Wow	1	100	1	100	0	0
Determine the distance the ball was from the flag on the green	25	81	100	100	None	-1	-100	-1	-100	-1	-100	Better than BIC	0	0	1	100	0	0
Could rest while waiting	26	0	13	0	None	-1	0	-1	0	-1	0	Nothing	-1	0	-1	0	-1	0
							-1088		-1113		-575			625		388		200

ferent. Each solution is evaluated against the best-in-class solution and is weighted using the IBT and IWT score. Each solution contains a concomitant risk/reward opportunity. Selecting the appropriate solution becomes a business judgment. We selected Solution A, since it represents the most significant product differentiation along with a reasonable risk/reward relationship.

Solution A addressed more of the "wow" requirements (3,11,12, and 24), for a total weighted score of 625 for all requirements. Solution B addressed three of these requirements (3, 24, and 25), for a total weighted score of 388 for all requirements, but required significantly higher investment and contained a greater element of risk. This was primarily due to addressing requirement 25. The solution incorporated a global positioning system, similar to the units currently available on golf carts, only portable. We determined that Solution B represented a higher risk than the potential returns would warrant. Solution C was not considered as a significant product differentiator because it addressed only two attractive requirements.

The completed requirements and solutions document in Figure A.11 is the culmination of all the steps in the MDPD process. This document clearly identifies the requirements to address when developing new product definitions. It "de-fuzzes" the fuzzy front end of product development with objective, fact-based criteria.

References

Introduction

1. Quoted in Stephanie Miles, "Behind Death of Divx Were Angry Customers," CNET's News.com, June 17, 1999.
2. Christopher L. Tyler, "Trendwest's William F. Peare, His Customer Focus Keeps Company Growing," *Investor's Business Daily*, April 19, 2001, p. A3.
3. Adjunct Professor Christopher Hart from the University of Michigan Business School studied seventeen divisions, ranging from cellular service to defense systems, of a multibillion-dollar company and confirmed the existence of this gap across all divisions. Senior management rated the company A- in terms of customer priority. As the level of employees dropped, perceptions and ratings of the company's performance in this area dropped as well, to a low of C-.
4. Gary Burchill, "Concept Engineering" (Ph.D. dissertation, Massachusetts Institute of Technology, June 1993).
5. Edward F. McQuarrie, *Customer Visits* (Newbury Park, Calif: Sage Publications, 1993).

Chapter 1

1. Lee Iacocca and William Novak, *Iacocca—An Autobiography* (New York: Bantam Books, 1984), pp. 64–65.

2. David W. Cravens, Gordon Greenley, Nigel F. Perry, and Stanley F. Slater, "Mapping the Path to Market Leadership," *Marketing Management,* Fall 1998, p. 31.

3. Responses were received from companies in the aerospace/defense, automotive, computer hardware and software, communications, components, electromechanical systems, electronic subsystems, financial, heavy machinery, instrumentation, housewares/small appliances, medical equipment, light assembly, chemical, food processing, service, software, and other industries.

4. Kim W. Chan and Renee Mauborgne, "Strategy, Value Innovation and the Knowledge Economy," *Sloan Management Review* 40 (Spring 1999), pp. 41–54.

5. George S. Day, *Marketing Driven Strategy: Processes for Creating Value* (New York: Free Press, 1990), p. 141.

6. Robert A. Lutz, *Guts: The Seven Laws of Business That Made Chrysler the World's Hottest Car Company* (New York: John Wiley & Sons, 1998), p. 13.

7. QFD is a method of product development that originated in Japan in the 1960s under the umbrella of Total Quality Control.

CHAPTER 2

1. The seven Ps of the title stand for "proper prior planning prevents pathetically poor performance."

2. According to a study conducted with the Committee on Engineering Design Theory and Methodology, National Research Council, "Improving Engineering Design: Designing for Competitive Advantage," 1991, p. 120.

3. Inbound marketing typically handles product definition and specification, while outbound marketing is concerned with product pricing and promotion.

CHAPTER 3

1. Using the Internet as a direct distribution channel raises a host of issues related to the online shopping customer, whether business-to-

consumer (B2C) or business-to-business (B2B). Chapter 12 of this book covers Internet distribution in more detail; however, the principles regarding the identification of the profile and needs of the customer still apply.

2. Eric von Hippel, Professor, Management of Technology, Massachusetts Institute of Technology, Sloan School of Management, "Managing Innovation Through Lead Users," program guide for video course.

3. Gary Hamel, *Leading the Revolution* (Boston: Harvard Business School Press, 2000),

CHAPTER 4

1. Dian Fossey, *Gorillas in the Mist* (Boston: Houghton Mifflin, 2000).
2. Ronald B. Lieber and Joyce E. Davis, "Storytelling; A New Way to Get Close to Your Customer," *Fortune*, February 3, 1997.
3. Ibid.
4. Ibid.

CHAPTER 5

1. Historical perspective of Consumer Acceptance of Products, Robert M. McMath, President, the New Products Showcase.
2. Christopher Power, Kathleen Kerwin, Ronald Grover, Keith Alexander, and Robert Hof, "Flops,"*Business Week*, August 16, 1993, pp. 76–82.
3. Ibid.
4. Ibid.
5. Jiro Kawakita, "The Original KJ Method" (Tokyo: Kawakita Research Institute, 1991). ("KJ Method" is trademarked in Japan.)
6. Shoji Shiba et al., *Step-by-Step KJ Method* (Cambridge, Mass.: Center for Quality Management, 1994).

CHAPTER 8

1. During a twelve-month period in 2000, Market Perspectives, Inc., conducted more than 200,000 survey interviews over the Internet.
2. The American Marketing Association (http://www.ama.org) and the Marketing Research Association (http://www.mra-net.org) are two sources that can provide assistance with survey sampling.
3. Based on typical quotes from Market Perspectives, Inc.
4. RSOR is a stack-ranking method that heavily weights the responses that receive a top ranking.
5. Noriaki Kano, Shinichi Tsuji, Nabuhiko Seraku, and Fumio Takerhashi, "Miryokuteki Hinshitu to Atarimare Hinshitsu" ("Attractive Quality and Must-Be Quality"), *Quality* 14(2) (Tokyo, Japan, Society for Quality Control, 1984).

CHAPTER 9

1. Moore's law projects that the price/performance of computer chips will double every eighteen to twenty-four months as a result of technological advances that enable greater miniaturization of semiconductor circuits. The law was postulated by and named after Gordon Moore of Intel Corporation.

CHAPTER 10

1. Edward de Bono, *Lateral Thinking: Creative Step-by-Step* (New York: HarperCollins, 1990).
2. Adjunct Lecturer Glen H. Mazur, University of Michigan College of Engineering, Theory of Inventive Problem Solving (TRIZ), http://www.personal.engin.umich.edu/gmazur/triz/.
3. Ellen Domb, first published in *Izobretenia, The Journal of the Altshuller Institute,* October 1999. http://www.triz-journal.com/archives.

4. Brian Deagon, "How Turnarounds Thrive Long-Term," *Investor's Business Daily,* March 27, 2001, p. A1.
5. Harley-Davidson press release on the Web at http://www.harley-davidson.com/company/news/.

Chapter 11

1. Coopers & Lybrand L.L.P., "Partnerships Pay Off for Growth Companies," *Industry Week,* February 17, 1997, p. 12.
2. Dell typically builds its computer systems to order within a week, then charges the customer's credit card on the same day the system ships by Federal Express. If Dell's suppliers of computer components are operating on a just-in-time delivery basis with typically thirty-day payment terms, Dell is using the customer's payments to cover the cost of inventory for the computer. Specifically, Dell gets paid before it has to pay its suppliers. If the volume is large enough and the firm is fast enough, it can operate on "negative cash flow."

Chapter 12

1. http://www.welcomeaddition.com/.
2. Miles D. White, chief executive officer, Abbott Laboratories, "Old Line Online: Transforming Traditional Companies Through E-Business," remarks by to The Executive Club of Chicago, September 27, 2000.
3. Xerox worked with the Massachusetts Institute of Technology to develop this site and with Modalis Research Technologies to host it.
4. Product Development Consulting benchmark study, "Time to Market," July 27, 1999. The study looked at twelve projects in seven R&D organizations in the office equipment market and measured time to market against time to profit. The participating organizations are leaders in their markets and provided quantitative data regarding their product development successes. Although the study was too small to offer scientific certainty, it is richly suggestive.

Index